About Allison Bottke's Setting Boundaries® books...

In 2008, author Allison Bottke launched her Setting Boundaries® series of books with the publication of *Setting Boundaries® with Your Adult Children*. That book has now sold more than 100,000 copies and has helped countless parents deal with the fallout of having adult children who have never taken responsibility for their own lives.

In the years since she wrote *Setting Boundaries® with Your Adult Children*, Allison has added these important titles to her series:

- *Setting Boundaries® with Your Aging Parents*
- *Setting Boundaries® with Difficult People*
- *Setting Boundaries® with Food*

This new book, *Setting Boundaries® for Women*, encourages you to take charge of your life by implementing boundaries in your workplace, home, church, and personal relationships. As in the previous books in the Setting Boundaries® series, Allison offers the valuable SANITY acronym to help you regain your sanity by setting appropriate boundaries and sticking to them.

Allison Bottke writes from the heart. She digs deep into her own experience with the complex issues people face daily. In Allison, you'll find a compassionate friend—and an author whose words can help you change your life.

High Praise for Allison Bottke's Setting Boundaries® books...

Setting Boundaries® for Women

I can so relate to all the Setting Boundaries® books written by Allison. I find myself on the pages of each book. They are so down to earth, practical, and applicable to living life today . . . especially this book!

Sharon Hill
prayer coach and author of the *OnCallPrayer*® Journal

If you are looking for a clear, concise, and effective way to improve your life, look no further. *Setting Boundaries® for Women* puts you in the driver's seat in life... Allison Bottke does an outstanding job of stripping away those stressors by offering a truly effective how-to guide on taming our most destructive emotions, which self-sabotage our peace and joy.

Tracey Mitchell, HDD
author of *Downside Up*

This is a must-read book for women today!

Dawn Irons, M.A., LPC

I found the entire book to be encouraging, leaving me with powerful tools in my arsenal to fight the temptation to live without boundaries. Thank you Allison for the SANITY plan!

Jill Angel
Soul Sisters Women's Ministry at Harvest Church, Fort Worth, TX

In *Setting Boundaries® for Women*, Allison reveals how boundaries are not only healthy, but fruit of a godly life. Allison helps us to identify the areas of our life that seem out of control, and gives simple, practical steps to implement healthy boundaries from a godly perspective, with real-life examples.

Dana Pollard
worship leader, songwriter, and recording artist of Grace for Eternity

I'm giving copies of this book to my girlfriends, mom, adult daughters, and the many women I care about in my life because I know this is a resource that can help us rise above our circumstances and live a more abundant life.

Ellie Kay
America's Family Financial Expert ® and best-selling author

Had I understood the content and action plans of *Setting Boundaries® for Women* in my earlier years, my life would have been healthier and happier...Keep this book handy—it's a vital resource to help you throughout your life.

Jennifer Strickland
speaker and author of *Beautiful Lies* and *Girl Perfect*

Setting Boundaries® for Women isn't just a book; it's a valuable tool to help break free of unhealthy conditioning and relationships that lack discipline. Allison Bottke delivers guidance in a digestible and practical manner for best application. It's a must-read for any woman!

Wendie Pett
talk show host and fitness and wellness expert

Setting Boundaries® for Women lays out an easy to follow guide to help navigate difficult and challenging relationships and events that are common to us all. Allison is an accomplished author, an inspirational voice, and a role model to real people, in a real world, with real challenges. Her words will bring hope, light, and peace to multitudes of lives!

Pastor Tiz Huch
DFW New Beginnings Church, Dallas, TX

Every page of *Setting Boundaries® for Women* made me think of someone who "needs to read this," then I realized she was already reading it. Me. This may be my favorite book yet in the life-changing Setting Boundaries series.

Donna Swan
Bible study group leader

I'm recommending this book to women who need to "stop and smell the roses." Don't just escape and have fun, but let boundaries open your spiritual eyes to why you've been blessed in the first place. See your value in God's eyes!

Ellen Kay
event planner and former flight attendant

I was forty years old before I learned there are such things as boundaries—much less that I could enforce them in my life as a daughter, wife, mom, and friend! If only I had Allison's book *Setting Boundaries® for Women* back then. Fortunate is the woman who reads this book now and puts the author's empowering principles into action... Pick up a copy for yourself and for a friend.

Karen O'Connor
author of *When God Answers Your Prayers: How God Comes Through in the Nick of Time*

Setting Boundaries® with Your Adult Children

This book will launch a brand-new beginning in your life. You may feel you are in a desert place as you struggle with a parenting crisis, but be alert! There's a stream in the wasteland—and you can begin making hope-filled choices that will forever change your future for the better.

Carol Kent
speaker and author of *When I Lay My Isaac Down* and *A New Kind of Normal*

No one knows better the pain of dealing with adult children who have lost their way than the parents of those without boundaries. Allison Bottke, writing through her own hurt and experience, has compiled a masterpiece of advice. She doesn't just tell you or show you how it's done. She walks along beside you.

Eva Marie Everson and Jessica Everson
authors of *Sex, Lies, and the Media*

Setting Boundaries® with Your Aging Parents

This book is written in the same spirit of hope, generosity, and faith that allowed the readers of Allison's first book in the Setting Boundaries® series to find a sane and safe place of recovery, optimism, and healing. It is an inspiring and important addition to the body of literature that addresses the problem and pain of adult children dealing with difficult parents. It is stunningly integrated with the importance of understanding that God is the ultimate authority, overriding both societal and psychological beliefs.

Mark Sichel, LCSW
author of *Healing from Family Rifts*

Setting Boundaries® with Difficult People

Well organized, powerfully written, thoughtful, challenging, and helpful for everyday living, this excellent volume is a keeper—a reference you'll refer to repeatedly as you encounter those inevitable aggravating relationships. Get it. Read it. Use it! And celebrate your less-stressful life.

Mary Hollingsworth
author and managing director, Creative Enterprises Studio

Allison Bottke has written a helpful and inspiring book on how to live with and manage difficult relationships at home, at work, in our community. So the task is to be kind, loving, grace filled and firm about how we wish to be treated. After reading this book you'll be well-equipped to do all of these things.

Karen O'Connor
author of *Help, Lord! I'm Having a Senior Moment*

Setting Boundaries® with Food

Many folks who have had difficult upbringings turn to something to fill them all the way up, such as food, sex, admiration, or success. Allison peels away the layers of why we reach for that piece of chocolate cake and why it seems to have power over us. And then she adeptly points us to the One who can fill us all the way up—Jesus.

Mary DeMuth
author of *Thin Places*

To all the special faith-filled women
God has placed in my life.

May our good and gracious Lord continue to
richly bless your lives as you have blessed mine.

I love those who love me,
and those who seek me find me.
PROVERBS 8:17

Setting *Boundaries*® for Women

ALLISON BOTTKE

HARVEST HOUSE PUBLISHERS
EUGENE, OREGON

Cover by Garborg Design Works, Savage, Minnesota

Cover photos © Chris Garborg

Allison Bottke is published in association with the literary agency of The Steve Laube Agency, LLC, 5025 N. Central Ave., #635, Phoenix, Arizona, 85012.

SETTING BOUNDARIES is a registered trademark of The Hawkins Children's LLC. Harvest House Publishers, Inc. is the exclusive licensee of the federally registered trademark SETTING BOUNDARIES.

This book contains stories in which the author has changed people's names and some details of their situations in order to protect their privacy.

SETTING BOUNDARIES® FOR WOMEN
Copyright © 2013 by Allison Bottke
Published by Harvest House Publishers
Eugene, Oregon 97402
www.harvesthousepublishers.com

Library of Congress Cataloging-in-Publication Data
    Bottke, Allison.
    Setting boundaries for women / Allison Bottke.
        pages cm
    Includes bibliographical references.
    ISBN 978-0-7369-4819-7 (pbk.)
    ISBN 978-0-7369-4820-3 (eBook)
    1. Christian women—Religious life. 2. Christian women—Conduct of life. 3. Interpersonal conflict —Religious aspects—Christianity. 4. Interpersonal relations—Religious aspects—Christianity. I. Title.
    BV4527.B68 2013
    248.8'43—dc23

2013010340

Printed in the United States of America
        13 14 15 16 17 18 19 20 21 / VP-JH / 10 9 8 7 6 5 4 3 2

Contents

Foreword by Suellen Roberts 11

Introduction 13

1. What Is SANITY? 21
2. What Are Boundaries, Anyway? 33
3. Are We Helping or Enabling? 47
4. Your Most Important Boundary 57
5. Why Setting Boundaries Is
   So Difficult for Christian Women 67
6. Encountering God's Word and Wisdom 75
7. When Boundaries Are Violated 81
8. Saying No Without Guilt 93
9. Expectations Can Be Exhausting 103
10. Personality, Emotions, and Motivations 115
11. Peace, Not Passivity 135
12. The Fruit of Healthy Boundaries 147
13. Go for It, Girl! 159

A Final Word from Allison 166
Appendix 1: The SANITY Support Creed 167
Appendix 2: Developing Your Action Plan 169
Appendix 3: Sample Letters to Send 189
Notes 193

Foreword

I sat glued to the compelling manuscript for *Setting Boundaries® for Women,* once again mesmerized by Allison's ability as a writer to weave together facts, stories, the Bible, and her own personal experiences into a masterful work that appeals to women from all walks of life.

We all experience life, its joys and tragedies, through our culture, our upbringing, and our walk of faith. However, each woman reading this will relate to this book in some vital way regardless of where you are in your life today.

Allison has always been willing to be up-front and personal about her journey in order to help others. God has used this transparency in a great way through all the books she has written, but particularly in the Setting Boundaries® series. Additionally, the highly valued opinion of others in the quotes throughout the book makes this a most exciting, informative, and insightful read.

My life is multifaceted, and I'm sure yours is as well. I'm the founder and president of the Christian Women in Media Association, and my blended family includes five children and eleven grandchildren. The joy of my life is my husband, Jimy, who is disabled, a godly man who served with Billy Graham for 20 years. I am his primary caregiver. I speak, write, and travel some. (I just returned from a trip to India!)

By God's grace, He helps me lead a Christ-centered and balanced life. However, it doesn't come easily. Making godly choices and learning to say no requires daily prayer. Ultimately, as we follow Christ and have a close relationship to Him, God supernaturally inspires us to walk in His will and His way for our lives.

I recently received a phone call from a prominent woman who was overwhelmed with her personal and professional commitments—a story I hear all too often. Most of the women I talk to and pray with struggle with this common issue of finding balance and peace.

How do we do it all and maintain sanity?

Ultimately, we must give our daily schedule to the Lord and cry out for His energy, passion, and purpose in order to do what He has called us to do.

Allison's approach to "doing it all" is fresh, and her insights are amazing and God-given. *Setting Boundaries® for Women* and the empowering and inspiring Six Steps to SANITY can definitely be life changers for women everywhere.

Suellen Roberts
Founder and President, Christian Women in Media Association
CWIMA.org

Introduction

You've picked up this book because you know you need boundaries in your life.

That's good. That's a start.

You've obviously seen an area or maybe several areas in your life that could benefit from boundaries. You should be complimented for acknowledging that need. Many women live their entire lives unaware of how much better life could have been if only they had seen their need for boundaries and implemented them. Some women may neglect to set boundaries because the idea seems limiting, restrictive. But rather than restricting us, properly defined boundaries with others and with ourselves actually increase our freedom to be the women God designed us to be.

Sometimes you can't control the unfolding panorama of external influences, circumstances, and situations. However, even then you can always control your responses and attitudes toward those circumstances as you also surrender them to God.

This is why boundaries can be so crucial. Boundaries properly set in place enable us to have control over our lives and our destiny.

"Control" is a word you'll see often in this book. That's because your goal in setting boundaries is to gain or regain healthy control over your own life whenever possible. Of course, sometimes you can't control the unfolding panorama of external influences, circumstances, and situations. However, even then you can always control your responses and attitudes toward those circumstances as you also surrender them to God. That will be key to remember. You may not be able to control every outward influence or circumstance in your life, but you *can* control the way you react or respond.

Exercising this type of self-control with the help of the Holy Spirit is life changing. Women who passively accept the barriers that keep them from appropriately controlling their lives remind me of Proverbs 25:28—"Like a city whose walls are broken through is a person who lacks self-control." Broken walls are like broken boundaries. The good news is that just as a city can rebuild broken walls, so too you can build the boundaries that will allow you to control your life and fulfill God's destiny for you.

To take control means also to stop sitting on the sidelines and stop viewing our lives as spectators. It means being intentional and rational in our actions and responses—not emotional.

For many Christian women, the notion of taking control has gotten a bad rap. After all, good Christian women are supposed to submissively cede control of their lives to someone else most of the time. Right?

Wrong. Christian women must be responsible for the decisions they make and the boundaries they set or don't set. But many women still hear a nagging question in the back of their minds. *Can I still be a good Christian woman if I set boundaries in my life?*

I would argue they're really asking, *Can I still be a good Christian woman if I take control of my life?*

My answer to that is a resounding yes! In fact, a "good Christian woman" *will* take control of her life under the guidance and leading of the Holy Spirit. Women, like men, have God-given gifts in this life, and God expects women to be good stewards of those gifts. To be a good steward will mean making responsible decisions and setting appropriate boundaries.

However, remembering these two valuable truths is important:

- Taking control is not the same as being controlling.
- Being assertive is not the same as being aggressive.

We take control of our lives by actively setting healthy boundaries. This is not a passive exercise. It takes involvement, commitment, and a willingness to be firm and loving. It requires an ability to identify where we need to change and to understand that we need to actively participate in that change. It includes respecting the boundaries other people have put in place.

As Christians, we need to know that setting healthy boundaries isn't about controlling every aspect of our environment. That's truly impossible. Rather, it's about knowing when and how we can and should exercise control by setting boundaries as the Holy Spirit guides us.

When we know something must change, we become responsible to take action and make the change—in our own lives, of course, not in someone else's, regardless how much we may think he or she needs to change. I hope that's why you bought this book—you're aware of your need, and now you just want direction and perhaps permission to move ahead.

Remember that setting boundaries isn't about convincing others to behave the way we think they should. It's about being very clear about our own limits, what we will and will not accept in our lives, and being able to back up these standards. It's about us behaving in a manner that protects our hearts, brings glory and honor to God, and builds our self-respect. It's about not relying on other people to give us approval or validate our feelings. It's about claiming our God-given spiritual authority.

People will grant us more and more respect and approval as we take control of our lives and set healthy boundaries.

Many of us don't fully grasp the value of boundaries until a crisis prompts us to do something fast. And a crisis is not the best time to make wise decisions. I've found that many of our crises could have been avoided if we had recognized the need for boundaries earlier— before the crisis occurred and we were forced into action.

And honestly, the more I observe the lives of women around me, the more certain I become that almost every challenge we women face is in some way related to boundaries. Either we have become lax with the effective boundaries that were already in place, or we have never really given much thought to how boundaries could be the remedy for the problems we face.

Before we launch into chapter 1 and consider my Six Steps to SAN-ITY, let's first take a few minutes for a personal inventory to help you clarify the areas in your life in the most need of boundaries. As you read, I'd like you to have a notebook close at hand. Throughout the next several chapters, I'll occasionally suggest you jot something in your notebook. It's best to find one that will fit in your purse or briefcase. In addition to jotting down notes, you should also use it as a journal as you read. Don't worry about spelling or story structure. This note-book is just a place for you to record your thoughts and your responses to my questions.

Relational Boundaries

1. Do you find yourself doing things for others (such as chores, errands, and caregiving) that you know they should be doing for themselves?

2. Do you do things for others so they will approve of you? In other words, are you a people pleaser?

3. Are you desperate to hold on to someone's affections—so much so that you compromise your principles? Do you do things you know are wrong in order to stay in someone's good graces?

4. Do you overlook or make excuses for someone's bad behavior or abuse?

5. Are you fearful of what life would be like if someone was not in your life?

6. Do you feel controlled by a relationship?

7. Do you have one or more difficult people in your life?

Family Boundaries

1. In healthy families, every person has responsibilities and roles to fill. Are you trying to fill other people's roles or just your own?

2. Do all your family members have assigned jobs? Are they held accountable for doing them?

3. Do your children have specific boundaries when it comes to curfew, homework, appropriate relationships with their friends, video games, and television?

4. Do you have time for yourself, or is every hour consumed with responsibilities? Should you share some of your responsibilities with others?

5. Do you feel tension in your family because you lack boundaries?

6. Do you feel tension with your in-laws or your parents?

7. Would you say your family life is out of control?

Work-Related Boundaries

1. Has your employer provided you with an accurate and reasonable job description?

2. Do you do work that you are not responsible to do?

3. Are you unreasonably called upon to stay late, take work home, or bend company rules?

4. Has anyone in your workplace become too personal with you?

5. Is anyone in your workplace not doing his or her work properly, causing extra work for you?

6. Has your job become your primary focus? Has it distracted you from more important things in your life?

7. Do you dread going to work?

Church-Related Boundaries

1. Do your responsibilities at church bring you joy, or do they cause stress?

2. At church, people often perform tasks that they feel no one else will do. Is that the case with you?

3. Do people sense your willingness to help and then expect you to take on new responsibilities?

4. Are you performing tasks at church that are not compatible with your gifts?

5. Does your work at church distract you from more important activities?

6. Does your involvement at church drain you spiritually, or does it invigorate you?

7. Have you become a Martha, or are you able to maintain a spirit like Mary's? (Read the story of Mary and Martha in Luke 10:38-42.)

Self-Related Boundaries

Setting boundaries for ourselves is sometimes the biggest boundary-related challenge we face. Boundaries we impose on ourselves can certainly be the hardest to enforce.

1. Do you expect attitudes from others that you don't display yourself?

2. Do you violate other people's boundaries? For instance, do you read your children's diaries or e-mail? Do you violate their privacy in the bathroom or bedroom? (The exception, of course, is when a mother's intuition gives her cause to worry about her child's safety and asking the child produces no results.)

3. When you're in a bad mood, do you take it out on others?

4. Do you respect yourself as God's child? Or do you constantly feel unworthy?

5. Are you too critical or even condemning of yourself because of a poor self-image?

6. Are you a good steward of your body, which God has given to you?

7. Is anyone abusing you physically, emotionally, or verbally?

8. Does anything from your past cause you to feel guilt, anger, pain, or insecurity?

Boundaries with Other Things

We usually think of boundaries with other people or with ourselves. But I want you to also consider the inanimate things in your life that may require boundaries.

1. How much time do you spend playing computer games, checking Facebook or other social networking sites, or just surfing the Web?

2. Are you prone to substance abuse?

3. Do you have any problems with money, such as overspending, not saving enough, or gambling?

4. How is your relationship with food?

5. Do you want to accumulate nicer clothes, shoes, cars, furniture, and so on, or are you content with what God has given you?

Often these issues with other things reveal a lack of boundaries with ourselves.

Of course, these six areas are not exhaustive. Perhaps other areas in your life warrant similar questions. If so, take a moment to think of some questions that will help you determine whether new or enhanced boundaries are necessary in these other areas. Write them in your notebook. You might consider your relationships with grandchildren, aging parents, adult children who refuse to grow up, or an ex-spouse who doesn't respect your boundaries. Other areas may occur to you as you keep reading.

These are my goals in the following pages:

1. To help you define boundaries in a way that's useful to you.

2. To help you identify areas of your life that need boundaries.

3. To help you actually implement the boundary decisions you know are necessary.

4. To help you change your perspective on control and find peace.

As you read, my prayer is that God will speak to you clearly about how you can benefit from appropriate boundaries, break free from bondage, and regain control of your life so you can move ahead to become the woman God has truly designed you to be. And *that* requires some SANITY!

1

What Is SANITY?

As we begin this journey together, I want you to get a grasp of my Six Steps to SANITY because I'll be referring to them throughout the book.

First, you need to know that the Setting Boundaries® books have been born out of my own experience. Out of sheer necessity, I've walked the walk that's led me to write these books.

The first book in the series, *Setting Boundaries® with Your Adult Children*, was a result of the pain I endured with my adult son, Christopher. Time after time I bailed him out of trouble, thinking I was helping him. The truth was, I was merely enabling my son to continue his inappropriate behavior. I was also driving myself crazy by trying to keep up the many other demands on my life. It simply wasn't working—at all.

Out of that sad experience, I developed the SANITY Steps, which helped me gain control of my life and gain a deeper understanding of God's plan and purpose for my life. As my readers have implemented them, they too have been helped in getting their lives back on track. I'm confident you'll be in that number too as you consider how these steps will help you implement the boundaries you need in your life.

In those early days with Christopher, I was living out the well-known definition of insanity: repeating the same behavior and expecting different results. I now call that running on the gerbil wheel of insanity. You've seen wheels that allow pet gerbils and hamsters to exercise but that take them nowhere regardless of how fast they run. That's essentially what the person without boundaries is doing. Running, hoping, praying, waiting for change to happen, and expecting a new result from the same old tactics but never employing the steps necessary for good change to occur. It took me awhile, but eventually I made the move I'm asking you now to make: Move off the gerbil wheel of insanity into the world of sanity—using the six SANITY Steps.

Think about your present situation. Surely it's not new to you. I'm guessing you've been on the gerbil wheel yourself and nothing has worked. You've repeated the same behavior and expected different results, only to be disappointed again and again.

The SANITY Steps

The following SANITY Steps are tools to help us initiate the good change in direction we need. These steps help us get into right relationships with God, with others in our lives, and with ourselves. They will help us to gain control and find peace.

By the way, as someone who has a relatively poor capacity to memorize things, I found it amazingly easy from the beginning to memorize these six steps, and I hope you will as well. At first, I had to consciously think about the steps, or the process. Now, they are almost as natural as breathing. In time, these steps will become second nature to you. And I can guarantee that when they do, your life will change.

S—Stop Your Own Negative Behavior

A—Assemble Supportive People

N—Nip Excuses in the Bud

I—Implement an Action Plan

T—Trust the Voice of the Spirit

Y—Yield Everything to God

S—Stop Your Own Negative Behavior

This first of the Six Steps to SANITY sounds the easiest in theory, yet it will be one of the most difficult in reality. In addition, the first step in any journey is often the hardest. That will probably be true for you, but without this crucial step you'll never arrive at your destination—a life of peace and destiny.

Our first "Stop" in this step is to silence our clamoring spirit and simply become still before God. The Bible tells us clearly in Psalm 46:10, "Be still, and know that I am God." That's hard for those of us on the gerbil wheel of insanity, but if we don't first become still before God, we will surely keep going in circles.

Stillness before God allows us to objectively identify the habits, behaviors, or attitudes we must stop in order to find sanity. It helps us know where we need to implement boundaries. It keeps us from lashing out in anger or frustration, which accomplishes nothing, as you surely know by now.

Having a still heart also allows us to move ahead and do what needs to be done. Merely identifying the things that must change is only part of the boundary-setting process.

Perhaps you have already identified some negative behaviors in your life that may be contributing to your problems. But if not, pray, look closely at your life, and ask others you trust to help you sort out any negative behaviors you must stop doing.

Applying the first of the Six Steps to SANITY in any challenging situation can bring illumination to our lives and enable us to see more clearly than we have for years—in all of our relationships. Accomplishing the following five "Stop" steps alone can be life changing.

1. Stop repeating your own negative behavior.

2. Stop ignoring your own personal issues (past and present).

3. Stop feeling guilty about taking control.

4. Stop ignoring the call to guard your heart.

5. Stop pushing God's will out of the picture.

In stopping our own negative behaviors, a good tool is self-talk. At times, my inner dialogue goes something like this. *Okay, Allison, this is an insane situation you're getting into. Don't go here. Don't get back on the gerbil wheel in this discussion, argument, or negotiation. Don't get caught up in these excuses and lies. Stop, step back, and be still—control your response and your tongue.*

As you stop the negative self-talk, you can begin to replace it with positive self-talk. *I can do this. I will stay in control of either the situation or my responses. God has empowered me to change my life!*

As we move through the book, you'll see examples of ways other women stopped their own negative behaviors that were contributing to their problems. You can do that too.

A—Assemble Supportive People

The second SANITY Step involves assembling a group of supportive people. We need others in both good and bad times. During our trials and tribulations, brothers and sisters in Christ can lend encouragement by listening, praying, and offering advice and an occasional shoulder to lean on.

We must sometimes emotionally distance ourselves from our circumstances and look at them objectively in order to gain a healthy perspective. When our strength runs low, it's often helpful to reach out to others who are willing to intervene on our behalf and hold us up. Making clear choices based on facts and not primarily on feelings is important when we're establishing new boundaries.

If this step sounds difficult to you, just remember that a support group doesn't need to be large. Your support group may be comprised of just three or four people. You may also find that a good support group for your boundary issue already exists. In most communities, it's easy to find groups that are supportive of those dealing with divorce, single parenting, unemployment, financial problems, health concerns, depression, or other issues. Check with area churches, community centers, and nonprofit organizations. Do an online search too. It's important to know you're not alone in whatever challenge you're facing. In turn, you may be able to offer your support to others facing the same challenges as you. Be careful, though, to make sure your support team shares your biblical values. Receiving well-meaning advice from someone who doesn't share your faith can lead to mixed signals and frustration.

In some situations, meeting one-on-one with a qualified Christian counselor may be necessary. Whether you meet with a licensed Christian counselor, a professional interventionist, or a recognized support group, it's vital that you surround yourself with supportive people.

For women who have been clinging to the fallacy that they must handle everything on their own, this can be a huge step toward freedom. One word of warning: If your boundary issues result from being in a relationship with an overbearing man, you may find this step all the harder. If such a controlling man is in your life, he may be opposed to or even openly hostile toward your attempts to establish boundaries. He may perceive your support group and even your whole notion of setting boundaries as enemies.

However, press on with caution. Other women have been in your spot and have summoned the courage to change, and you can too.

A Word About Abusive Control

You may not be dealing with abuse and excessive control. Not every woman who has trouble saying no is a victim of violence. There are many reasons why we get stuck in life, and not all are related to abuse. However, the issue of violated boundaries—physical, verbal, emotional, mental, or spiritual—plays a significant part in the lives of many women who struggle to understand and set boundaries. For many women, the first step in setting healthy boundaries will be to address issues of violated boundaries. That is why I have devoted an entire chapter to this very real and sometimes dangerous topic.

In such a case, your "Stop" step will include no longer believing that you deserve to be treated badly. You don't. And supportive people will be a huge help to you in this too. At times they may need to simply reaffirm your own worth as you work to identify or undo the damage done by others who are hurting you.

N—Nip Excuses in the Bud

As we have just seen, setting boundaries can be fraught with obstacles. Those obstacles include excuses—either from you or from the person with whom you've set a boundary. In such cases, we need this third SANITY Step: *Nip Excuses in the Bud.* These excuses are often merely justifications of negative behavior.

Excuses can sound like this: "He didn't mean to hit me. He had a rough day at work." Or "My daughter isn't involved with drugs. She just got hooked up with the wrong crowd." Or "My coworker's flattering comments are harmless. He's not really sexually harassing me." Or how about this excuse? "My life is so busy right now, I can't read a newspaper column, let alone my Bible."

You'll also need to nip accusations in the bud—accusations from your inner accuser or from those with whom you've set boundaries. "You're being unreasonable!" Or "Why are you so legalistic?" Or "Other moms let their daughters stay out late!" Get used to hearing things like that…and nip them in the bud. Just be sure your boundaries are reasonable (more about that later).

Regardless of the excuses or the accusations that have been plaguing you for months or years, now is the time to nip them in the bud. *No more excuses.*

I—Implement an Action Plan

The fourth Step, the development of an action plan, has been a critical component for those who have read other Setting Boundaries® books, such as parents of adult children or folks struggling with difficult people, dysfunctional (or toxic) aging parents, or even with food.

This step involves identifying and prioritizing your challenging areas, determining what actions need to be taken to implement change, and carefully considering the consequences. If we wait until a boundary needs to be set or one has been overstepped before deciding how we're going to reply in a different way, we're likely to default to our old behavior. We may say yes when we should say no. In fact, a classic one-liner goes something like this: Stress is what happens when your insides are saying, "I can't do this!" and your mouth is saying, "Of course I would be happy to..."

For example, here is a good plan of action to implement immediately if you tend to say yes when you should say no. Simply (and truthfully) say, "I can't give you an answer right now. I'll have to pray about it and get back to you." Then *do* pray about it. And in your prayers, don't try to justify saying yes. Truly let God speak to you.

An action plan becomes a much more powerful tool when we not only develop it but also record it on paper. The power of the written word is strong indeed, and writing out your plan adds strength and clarity to your resolve. It's part of the process to help you see yourself in a different light and to develop new habits.

We may be the only ones who see these plans, but we need to write them out nonetheless. Implementing a plan of action is all about taking action. We can talk all we want about finding SANITY, but until we're willing to do the necessary work to change, very little will change. This is where the rubber meets the road. We'll spend more time on your action plan in a later chapter.

T—Trust the Voice of the Spirit

The essence of finding peace and SANITY is in the intentional development of our faith. God can lead us or sometimes restrain us in our decision-making process. God *does* answer prayer.

This practice of asking God to lead or restrain me didn't come naturally, and it's still something I must do intentionally in order to rely more on God and less on myself. We can do that only by consistently asking Him to reveal truth to our hearts and minds through the Voice of the Spirit. We can rely on the promise in Proverbs 3:5-6 as we take this step: "Trust in the LORD with all your heart and lean not on your own understanding; in all your ways submit to him, and he will make your paths straight."

How does God "make your paths straight"?

He does it by giving you spiritual wisdom and discernment as you walk in relationship with Him.

It begins with trust. If we trust in the Lord with all our heart, we must also trust what He teaches us about the power of the Holy Spirit.

> And I will ask the Father, and he will give you another advocate to help you and be with you forever—the Spirit of truth. The world cannot accept him, because it neither sees him nor knows him. But you know him, for he lives with you and will be in you (John 14:16-17).

There are two ways God usually speaks to us: through prompting and through teaching. Promptings are inspirations or inner urges that show us what to do, with whom, and when. Teachings (often from sermons, talks, or books) help us relate properly to specific situations, providing clarification and attitude adjustment. In short, promptings tend to enhance spiritual intuition or insight. Teachings help us develop and refine our spiritual perspective, showing the way to stable happiness.

When we listen to and follow the inner voice of truth and wisdom and conquer the demons of habitual poor choices and responses, we can celebrate a true victory!

However, this kind of listening requires inner discipline. With practice, this spiritual intuition becomes more natural as we understand God's truth as revealed in His Word. If this is new to you, a very good way to begin listening to God is to start with a short reading from the Bible. Read a couple of psalms perhaps. Then let that lead you into praying about your situation. Next, spend some time listening to God's direction for you. His guidance may, in fact, come from the very words you've read from the Bible. If you think you've heard from God but you're not sure, run your direction from God by a trusted member of your support team.

Y—Yield Everything to God

The final SANITY Step is to *Yield Everything to God*, or "let go and let God." When the "letting go" part has been accomplished in our heart and "letting God" has become our focus, something amazing begins to happen. We feel free! We may not even realize how our fears had imprisoned us until those fears are gone.

To be sure, letting go can be scary. We must let go of unrealistic expectations, negative emotions, and lies of the enemy. When we choose to *Yield Everything to God*, we make a choice that will forever change our lives.

Applying the SANITY Steps

We can't put a timetable on God's plan for our lives, but we can put a timetable on when we're going to intentionally start making the changes (setting the boundaries) needed to bring about the change we seek.

Today we have numerous procedures, systems, and tools we can depend on in difficult situations—CPR to restart a heart, antibiotics to fight infection, and extinguishers to control fire. Alcoholics Anonymous and other 12-step programs help people who struggle with alcoholism and other addictions. Celebrate Recovery focuses on God's healing and redemptive power to deliver people from a multitude of challenges. It uses Eight Recovery Principles (based on the Beatitudes) and 12 biblical steps of recovery. Virtually everywhere we look today, God has provided help for us to specifically address our needs. The choice to embrace this help is ours to make.

We're really without excuse when we don't use the resources God has provided so we can experience all He has for us. We sometimes lack the courage to do the hard thing right in front of us. Boundaries work only when they're implemented. Reading this book will be helpful but only if you apply what it says. Otherwise, it's just another book. Let it be more than that.

The SANITY Steps appear on a separate page at the end of this chapter. I encourage you to make a copy of this page and post it somewhere visible. The beauty of SANITY is that anyone can follow the steps regardless of the situation. Posting the list where others may see it can open the door to discussions about setting boundaries and taking God-honoring control. For example, a husband who is facing a challenge on his job, a child who is dealing with a bully at school, or a roommate who is grappling with a drug-addicted boyfriend can all use the tools of SANITY to make better choices that can bring about effective change in their lives.

With a basic understanding of the six steps you'll be taking toward SANITY, let's take a look at the subject of boundaries.

Six Steps to SANITY

S — Stop Your Own Negative Behavior

A — Assemble Supportive People

N — Nip Excuses in the Bud

I — Implement an Action Plan

T — Trust the Voice of the Spirit

Y — Yield Everything to God

in·san·i·ty
/in ˈsanitē/
n: doing the same thing
and expecting different results

SettingBoundariesBooks.com

SANITY Step One

Stop Your Own Negative Behavior

Starting now, I will…

- Stop repeating the same responses and expecting different results.
- Stop my own destructive patterns, behaviors, and attitudes.
- Stop ignoring my own personal issues.
- Stop being alone in my pain.
- Stop pretending things are going to be fine if I continue as I have been.
- Stop putting off the changes I must make.
- Stop feeling guilty.
- Stop demanding that other people change.
- Stop making excuses for other people's negative behavior and choices.
- Stop engaging in arguments, debates, or negotiations.

SettingBoundariesBooks.com

2

What Are Boundaries, Anyway?

When we hear the word "boundary," we instantly think of a limit or a border, something that divides entities from each other, such as cities, states, or countries. We know where our property ends and our neighbor's property begins because of the boundary-defining fence between our yards. In sports, when a ball crosses a boundary line, it is no longer in play. It's out of bounds. It has exceeded its limits.

Sometimes people go out of bounds too. We all do at one time or another. We're human. This becomes a problem when people are consistently out of bounds or when their actions are dangerous or threatening. That's when we need to implement change.

Besides these common physical boundaries, we also have psychological and relational boundaries. We have boundaries in our personal lives and in our professional lives.

Rather than confining us or limiting us, boundaries often do just the opposite. They free us to do things in life that really matter. They show us more clearly where not to spend our energies (or waste them).

Boundaries, then, can protect yards, ball games, citizens, rights, and lives. They can even protect our hearts from relationships that can harm us emotionally. Without boundaries our lives would tend toward chaos.

Physical Boundaries

Physical boundaries protect your body, your sense of personal space, and your privacy. They can include clothes, shelter, safety, money, space, noise, and many other things.

Your physical boundaries need to be strong in order to protect you from harm. For example, if you have a deep wound and it goes untreated, you expose yourself to infection, which can have life-threatening consequences. Protecting this aspect of your physical boundaries is essential for your health and well-being.

Distance is another physical boundary. Has someone ever approached you to discuss an issue and stood too close? Your immediate and automatic reaction is to take a step back in order to reset your personal space. This sends a nonverbal message to the person that when he or she stands so close, you feel an invasion of your personal space. If the person continues to move closer, your next step might be to verbally protect your boundary by telling him or her to stop crowding you. Again, you're protecting your personal physical space by setting your boundary. Some of us don't know how or when to take a step back. Some of us are afraid to.

Here are some other examples of physical boundary invasions.

- inappropriate touching, such as making unwanted sexual advances

- physical abuse, such as pushing, shoving, slapping, punching, or beating

- looking through others' personal letters, documents, purse, dresser drawers, and so on

- not allowing others their personal space—barging into your bathroom at home without knocking, for example

Just as physical boundaries define who may touch us, how someone may touch us, and how physically close we will allow someone to be, psychological boundaries define where our feelings end and other people's begin. Many of us have no understanding of this differentiation.

Psychological Boundaries

Psychological boundaries protect the thinking part of who we are—what we put into our heads and what goes on inside there. This is the realm of our emotions and thoughts, our will, intellect, mind, worldview, and pattern of thinking. It's what we carry in our mind, our knowledge, wisdom, experience, memories, reflections, speculations, vocabulary, and opinions. In some cases, it includes the lies we have believed.

Psychological boundaries are important. They protect our sense of self-esteem and our ability to separate our feelings from the feelings of others. For example, do we take responsibility for our feelings and needs and allow others to do the same? Or do we feel overly responsible for other people's feelings and needs, and neglect our own? In short, do we try to ensure that someone is happy?

> When we have weak emotional boundaries, we are like people who are caught in the midst of a hurricane with no protection. We expose ourselves to being controlled by others' feelings, and we can end up feeling bruised, wounded, and battered.

Are we able to say no to a request that we know warrants a no? Are we compulsive people pleasers? Do we become upset simply because others around us are upset? Do we mimic other people's opinions just so we don't rock anyone's boat? The answers to these questions help define our internal "property lines"—our psychological and emotional boundaries.

When we have weak emotional boundaries, we are like people who are caught in the midst of a hurricane with no protection. We expose ourselves to being controlled by others' feelings, and we can end up feeling bruised, wounded, and battered.

The Dynamic Duo

Our physical and psychological boundaries define the way we interact with others and the way we allow others to interact with us. Without boundaries, others could touch us in any way they wanted, do whatever they wished with our possessions, and treat us in any way they desired. In addition, we would believe everyone else's bad behaviors are our fault, take on everyone else's problems as our own, and feel as if we have no rights of our own. In short, our lives would be chaotic.

Does this describe your life or the life of someone you know? If so, implementing boundaries can help bring freedom.

Establishing and integrating healthy physical and psychological boundaries allows us to live authentically. Yet making this critical integration can be one of the most difficult things we ever do, especially if we've lived for years in a disconnected sort of oblivion about the part these boundaries play in our lives.

In order to set healthy boundaries, we must develop emotional authenticity. We must do some deep self-introspection and address significant life issues at the core of our being—issues such as pain from our past, codependency, depression, domestic violence, childhood abuse, alcoholism, divorce, unhappy marriages, addictions, and bipolar disorders.

Three Types of Boundaries

Let's consider three other kinds of boundaries. Each of these three categories can be further broken down into temporary boundaries or permanent boundaries. A temporary boundary is one that most likely has a short-term objective in mind. Permanent boundaries are usually more serious.

Preventative Boundaries

These are boundaries you put in place before situations spiral out of control. For example, imagine giving your nine-year-old son a new video game. You're aware these games are time consuming and sometimes even addictive, so you may set a boundary regarding how much time your son may spend playing the game. This is to protect him from a danger he may not be aware of—that of losing himself in another world to the exclusion of his chores, homework, and relationships.

Here's another example of a preventative boundary. Let's say your doctor informs you that you're prediabetic. You'll probably need to change your diet and increase your exercise. That means you'll need to implement a preventative boundary by not eating certain foods in order to prevent diabetes.

You may see the need for developing preventative boundaries in relationships too. For example, many women have been so caught up in the excitement of meeting potential mates, they didn't establish preventative boundaries early on in relationships. As a result, they crossed lines that they never should have.

Of course, it's awkward to go out with a man, be seated at a nice table in a romantic restaurant, and say, "Okay, let's talk about setting up some preventative boundaries in our new relationship." That will surely end the date on the spot. Instead, set the boundary in your own mind before the evening begins. In addition to protecting promising relationships, these boundaries will likely filter out the men you don't want in your life anyway. When a man respects you for saying no, the relationship holds promise. If you're a single woman and you occasionally go out with new male acquaintances, consider writing out (in your private journal) the preventative boundaries you're establishing for new relationships. Then stick to those boundaries.

Protective Boundaries

A protective boundary is closely related to a preventative boundary but more overtly designed to protect you from harm. It's usually more serious than a preventative boundary and is sometimes required because a preventative boundary was never set in place.

For example, you might decide to stop seeing a man who didn't respect your preventative boundary. Parents of adult children may have to establish protective boundaries with adult children who are consistently disrespectful or even threatening. A legal restraining order is an extreme protective boundary.

Restorative Boundaries

Earlier I mentioned that boundaries can be temporary or permanent. A restorative boundary is a temporary boundary. Its purpose is to restore a relationship or a privilege. For example, if your teenage daughter has been out with friends every night and her grades are falling, you could institute a temporary boundary (a curfew) to bring her grades up. When her grades are satisfactory and you feel you can fully trust her, you might relax the boundary or eliminate it altogether.

We need healthy boundaries in virtually every relationship we have. Let's take a look at two of those relationships.

Boundaries in Marriage

Many starry-eyed young brides marry assuming they will live happily ever after. That really does happen in some marriages. But with divorce rates sky-high (even among Christians), we know that many brides will eventually face some disappointments in their marriages. In fact, according to an old saying, men marry women hoping they'll never change, but they always do. Women marry men hoping they'll change, but they never do.

What is the result? Many women discover that they need to clarify or develop some acceptable and healthy boundaries. A wife can be motivated to establish healthy boundaries when her husband...

- is a workaholic who neglects his role in the family
- makes critical decisions affecting the entire family without input from his wife
- doesn't communicate with his wife and/or children
- physically or mentally abuses his wife and/or children

- is caught up in viewing Internet pornography
- has entered into an affair with another woman
- doesn't do his share of work around the house

Some of these examples are clearly more serious than others. For instance, a husband who is having an affair has already violated a boundary that God set and that the husband vowed to uphold. God's command and the husband's vow are both permanent boundaries.

So what does a wife do when she needs to establish boundaries with her husband? It depends on the severity of the problem, her ability to rationally communicate her needs in this situation, the husband's willingness to accept responsibility for the problem, and the wife's willingness to forgive and employ restorative boundaries.

Let's say a husband is addicted to porn. He and his wife might agree on a restorative boundary by setting up the computer in the living room or some other less private place. (Parents should also consider this as a preventative boundary with their children.)

However, sometimes simply discussing the issue rationally with firmness and love can be very difficult to do.

Admittedly, setting boundaries with a spouse can be risky. A husband may feel defensive if his wife issues what he sees as ultimatums in their marriage. Unfortunately, this is what many women do when they feel pushed to the edge and finally decide that enough is enough.

Setting healthy boundaries in a firm and loving manner requires the ability to conduct open, honest, and rational (not emotional) communication. And here's the rub. The ability to verbally articulate our needs in a rational manner (that is, to communicate) doesn't come naturally or easily if we have boundary-related challenges.

Let's paint a hypothetical scenario using the issue of Internet pornography.

Let's say you've discovered that your husband has been spending several hours almost every evening viewing pornography on the computer. Unexpected charges showed up on your credit card, or you caught him in the act, or maybe he admitted what he was doing. And let's say that this goes against your values and morals, that you consider what he is doing as a sin. Let's take it even further and say that your marriage is at stake. You've just finished dinner, and now he says he is going to unwind in his man cave. Which of the three responses below will be not only the most effective but also the most God-honoring?

- "Oh…okay…I guess I'll finish the dishes" (passiveness and denial).

- "I know exactly what you're going to go do! Stop lying to me! How can you watch that disgusting filth on our computer? What's the matter with you? I'm sick to my stomach, and it has to stop! Now!" (aggression and accusation).

- "Before you sit down at the computer tonight, I need to tell you that I know what you're watching. I called the bank to confirm some charges I couldn't explain, and a lot of things began to make sense to me. I love you, and I value our marriage, but I need you to know that your actions aren't acceptable to me. I'm your wife, not your mother, so I'm not going to tell you to stop what I think is a sin, although I'm praying that you will stop and seek help. It's not up to me to make you change, but I can't condone this in our marriage. I've been praying that God would give me wisdom and discernment as I approached this subject with you. I'd like for us to sit down and talk about this" (self-control and rationality).

The first two responses are typical—and understandable. The third response, however, requires considerable strength and self-control. It requires the clarity of conviction that comes when we know our identity in Christ. It requires an understanding of our emotions, our motivations, and our needs. It requires a commitment to respond appropriately when people hurt us with their unacceptable behavior.

It requires that we know our worth in God's eyes and are willing to walk in His plan and purpose for our lives.

Being able to respond in this manner is possible when we follow the SANITY Steps. It's even easier when we have developed a written plan of action that helps us identify the issues we want to address, the actions we might take, and the consequences of those actions. We could also prepare by determining how we are going to approach the person and how we will articulate our needs.

Remember, we take appropriate control of our lives with intentional, rational actions, not emotional reactions.

It's important to say that there is no guarantee the third response is going to bring about immediate change or any change at all. It could be met with defensiveness, anger, denial, or indifference. However, it has the best chance of leading to healthy protective and restorative boundaries. In this situation, consulting a professional Christian counselor would be helpful. The wife would need to be prepared for her next step in the event this initial response didn't bring about change or resolution.

Boundaries in the Workplace

Many women also need boundaries in the workplace. Common violations here include inappropriate advances from coworkers or bosses, undefined work expectations, and enmity with coworkers. Thankfully, most reputable workplaces now have written codes of conduct covering sexual harassment or inappropriate overtures. When no such policy exists, consider encouraging your manager or your human resources department to implement one.

As for undefined expectations regarding the workload, make sure you're clear about who in the office needs a boundary. Many companies have written job descriptions. If none exist, you can politely suggest to your supervisor that a job description would help you work more efficiently. Yet even this action may have consequences, so it's important to pray for wisdom and discernment.

But not all such situations require boundaries for the employer. Sometimes the problems can be traced to a need for a personal boundary. For a good example, let's consider Susan.

Susan has worked as an administrative assistant in a midsize law firm for three years. With her two children married and starting families of their own, she initially took the part-time position to keep busy and to augment her husband's retirement income. When she began, the staff included two attorneys, one receptionist, and Susan. Now there are five attorneys, one receptionist, two administrative assistants, and a part-time file clerk. Susan now works full-time and assists three of the attorneys, including Mr. Nelson, the owner of the firm. In addition to her administrative responsibilities, she also handles the office management, which consists of payroll, accounting, supply ordering, and much more. She wants to be a helpful team player and seldom says no to anything requested of her, and when new administrative projects arise, she's often the first to volunteer.

However, over the past year, Susan's responsibilities have increased and her work has doubled. She often works late into the evening and has missed church the past three Sundays in order to go to the office and catch up before the week begins. Still, she never seems to get ahead. Mr. Nelson has been good to her, providing yearly raises, bonuses, and paid vacations. He sincerely appreciates her capabilities, and Susan doesn't want to let him down.

In fact, because she's agreed to help with so many additional projects, she has missed most of her grandson's soccer games this season and her granddaughter's first dance recital. Her husband has begun to do some of the things on his own they had talked about doing together when he retired, such as golfing and visiting museums. They barely see each other these days, and when they do speak, tension fills the air. Susan's life is beginning to spin out of control. What should she do? What kind of boundaries will help, and whose boundaries should they be?

When Susan heard about my SANITY Steps, she sat down and wrote out her personal goals, how she planned to reach them, and what was hindering those goals. She quickly realized implementing some boundaries would help her as well as the entire office staff.

As Susan continued to consider her situation, she realized that the boundaries she needed to establish were mostly boundaries for herself. Mr. Nelson wasn't overstepping his boundaries—he was taking his cues from Susan. When she offered to help, he assumed she had the time and ability to handle the extra projects in addition to her other responsibilities. He didn't know that most of the time she took on additional projects because she needed approval and was afraid to say no. Until Susan told her boss she was overwhelmed by the workload, he had no idea he was crossing a boundary because Susan had never established one.

After writing out her personal goals and realizing her need for boundaries, Susan knew she needed to talk with Mr. Nelson. She realized that she alone was responsible for her predicament. No one had forced her to take on so much extra work. She had willingly accepted or even initiated the additional projects. Now, to return her marriage to its rightful priority, she had to tell Mr. Nelson that she couldn't follow through with many of the projects and would no longer be able to work overtime.

She apologized to her husband for allowing her job to take precedence over their marriage. They discussed her decision to meet with her boss, and they prayed together about it. They even looked at all the possible consequences to her decision, including losing her job, although she prayed earnestly that wouldn't happen. She wrote down what she would say to Mr. Nelson and practiced her statement. When she met with Mr. Nelson, she came to the table as a calm and rational employee with an authentic heart.

Her attitude and behavior made all the difference in the world. Mr. Nelson accepted her explanation and respected her desire to initiate proper boundaries by developing mutually agreed upon job descriptions for Susan and the rest of the staff (which, it turned out, brought relief to the entire office).

Tracing Susan's actions, we see that she first had to take the "S" Step in SANITY: *Stop Your Own Negative Behavior*. Susan had to stop saying yes to new projects. She had to stop pretending she could accomplish everything on her plate at work. She had to stop missing church in order to go to the office to catch up on work. She had to stop giving her job a higher priority than her marriage. And she had to stop putting off a one-on-one meeting with Mr. Nelson to discuss her workload and hours.

We can easily get caught up in our own activities without considering God's will, so we need to take control by acting in accordance with His plan. In her heart, Susan knew she needed more of God's will in her life than she was presently living. She knew God wanted her to remain a committed wife to the husband she loved. She knew God wanted her to be a present and loving grandmother. She knew she wanted to serve God through participating at church more often. With a certainty of God's will as her starting point, Susan knew it was time to talk to her boss about her increasing job responsibilities. When Susan stopped all the busyness and prayed for direction, her spirit was filled with peace about taking control of her life by establishing boundaries regardless of the outcome.

Knowing God's will is vital. Have you ever prayed to discover exactly what God wants from you while you're here? You can start with the obvious callings He's given you. Are you a wife? That's a calling (just as being a husband is a calling for many men). Are you a mother? That's a calling from God too. Are you a professional woman with a career or occupation? That can certainly be a calling. Your work at church can also be a calling.

Susan's work at Mr. Nelson's office may be included in God's calling on her life, but it's neither her only calling nor her primary calling.

The SANITY Steps can help us learn to respond rationally in firm and loving ways to…

- our spouses
- our adult children
- our parents and in-laws
- our family
- our friends
- our coworkers
- our employers and managers
- our neighbors
- our church family

Taking Control

Here are some questions to ask yourself based on this chapter. Write your answers in your notebook, and remember to jot down the date at the top of the page.

1. Have you seriously thought about your personal boundaries? Are they necessary, or are your challenges all related to other people or things?

2. What is your primary calling at this point in your life? (It can change over the course of a woman's lifetime.)

3. Are you presently able to fulfill that primary calling?

4. Later in this book we will identify where God is convicting us to set boundaries. But first, list your top five priorities in your notebook. Under each one, list the main obstacle or obstacles that keep you from doing your best to honor those priorities.

Are We Helping or Enabling?

As contemporary women, we have many responsibilities and tasks. We are single, married, divorced, or widowed. We are students, educators, volunteers, or retirees. We are employees or employers. We may be homemakers, wives, parents, and grandparents. We could be caregivers of our aging parents or our spouses with health challenges. Some of us are raising our grandchildren.

We take care of husbands, kids, houses, cars, cats, and dogs. We cook, shop, handle the budget, pay bills, and conduct household maintenance and upkeep. Many women do all of this while also working outside the home full-time or part-time.

We wear many hats, yet underneath all of this doing, being, and accomplishing, we are daughters of God, called to guard our hearts, fulfill the purpose of God, and fulfill our purpose as His ambassadors, His representatives. That is the core of who we are.

How about you? Think about your own situation. Ask yourself some questions you may never have asked before.

- Does God want me to take responsibility for individuals in my life who aren't taking responsibility for themselves?

- Does God want me to pull out my checkbook every time my adult child gets into a financial bind?

- Does God want me to endure fear and pain under physical, verbal, or emotional abuse?

- Does God want me to put my health at risk by assuming responsibilities that aren't really mine, simply because I've not been able to say no?

- Does God want me to live with the spirit of guilt, anger, shame, or fear because of my inability to set healthy boundaries and take control of my life? Or does He want me to take responsibility for the life and assignments He has given me?

The Difference Between Helping and Enabling

I've found that many women are in challenging relationships that have weak or nonexistent boundaries because they haven't understood the difference between helping and enabling.

When I wrote *Setting Boundaries® with Your Adult Children*, I came down hard on parents who enable—parents like me. There was no doubt in my mind that many parents in pain needed a wake-up call. It was time to stop tiptoeing around the truth. We were playing important roles in the dysfunctional dramas of our adult children's lives.

I knew these parents' journey to find SANITY wasn't going to be easy, but I knew it was possible because I wasn't asking parents to go anywhere I hadn't already been.

When I finally realized the many ways I had contributed to my son's problems by enabling his behavior, I had nowhere to go but up. I had reached the end of the line.

Likewise, when a woman finally recognizes the difference between helping and enabling, she takes a critical step toward setting appropriate boundaries in her life. All the more so when she realizes she has been enabling others.

Helping is doing something for someone that he is not capable of doing himself.

Enabling is doing something for someone that he could and should be doing himself.

An enabler recognizes that a negative circumstance is regularly occurring and yet continues to help the person continue his or her detrimental behaviors. Simply, *enabling creates an atmosphere in which others can comfortably continue their unacceptable behavior.*

As difficult as it may be to hear, some of us women have surely played a part in many of our challenging relationships and situations. We've allowed others (husbands, employers, employees, church leaders, aging parents, adult children, minor children, neighbors, and so on) to overstep their boundaries. We've excused their unacceptable behavior by saying, "He'll never change," or "That's just her personality," or "I'll help out because I love him," or "If I don't do this, no one else will."

We may think we're helping, but we're actually enabling. And by enabling, we're hurting the other person—and ourselves.

Some of us have our own personal issues with weak, nonexistent, or violated boundaries. When we become parents, we often develop a myopic focus on our children. We may become first-rate enablers—partly because we think we're helping our children and partly because we'll do anything to keep from looking at our own lives. The older our children get, the more we forget the difficulties of our past, and we settle into a people-pleasing or codependent way of life that becomes as normal to us as breathing.

In *Setting Boundaries® with Your Adult Children*, I focused quite a bit on adult children who take advantage of their parents. These adult children take, take, and take because their parents give, give, and give. The parents have grossly confused helping with enabling, particularly when they come to the rescue with their checkbooks. This is one of the primary issues in the adult-child enabling epidemic sweeping our country today.

Unfortunately, the enabling component can exist in any relationship, and it's becoming more prevalent as lines of responsibility and expectation become blurrier.

One day, a distraught woman called a radio station when I was being interviewed about my book *Setting Boundaries® with Difficult People*. She said she frequently volunteered in the church kitchen for the weekly potluck luncheon and couldn't understand how disrespectful some of her fellow volunteers were. They often shirked their responsibilities, which left her consistently picking up after them on Sundays. She was soft-spoken, articulate, and considerate but clearly perplexed.

Assuming the other ladies were clear about their responsibilities in the first place, this woman was having trouble seeing her part in the dynamic. By choosing to consistently pick up after them, she created an atmosphere where the other volunteers could comfortably continue their irresponsible behavior. She thought, *If I don't do it, no one else will.* Her helping was actually hurting.

Keep in mind that enabling can be active or passive. In my case, I was actively enabling my son by doling out money and doing whatever I could to save his skin time after time. We enable passively when we simply let unacceptable behavior continue without responding. When a male coworker makes his third sexual innuendo in your direction and you ignore him, you're enabling him to continue by not taking a stand.

When we choose to accept (either actively or passively) unacceptable behaviors (such as disrespectful behavior, manipulation, abuse, irresponsibility, lying, addictions, and stealing), we're setting a pattern in our relationships that is difficult (but not impossible) to change.

Some people don't care if they overstep boundaries. Others simply don't realize what they are doing. Still others take their cues from what we tell them or don't tell them. That's why making our boundaries clear is so important.

Why is setting healthy boundaries so difficult for so many of us? Let's ask ourselves the following questions. Be brutally honest with your responses.

• Why do we say yes when we should say no?

- Why do we think it's okay to control other people's lives (or situations and circumstances) but not our own?
- Why have we accepted unacceptable behavior from others?
- Why do we feel responsible for things that aren't our responsibility?
- Why are we often afraid to set boundaries?

Some of us don't even realize the negative habits we've developed that keep us from establishing boundaries. Is this because of the emotional baggage we carry?

Are we emotionally needy and desperate for the approval of others? If that's the case, (and if we don't have adult children to enable) often we'll find someone to take care of, such as spouses, parents, siblings, or coworkers. In our desire to be needed, we rush to take care of a person or situation. But many times, we're actually handicapping those around us who need to accept their own responsibilities or the consequences of their own actions. Remember the difference between helping and enabling: We *help* people by doing things they can't do for themselves. We *enable* people by doing things they should be doing for themselves. Therefore, we must always ask ourselves, *Am I helping or enabling?*

Sadly, I recall another example of enabling...

My mother loved crafting. She was always making something with yarn, beads, glitter paint, and fabric. Her rubber-stamp collection was amazing, and she used it to decorate greeting cards, bookmarks, and stationery. Now that she's gone, I'm so glad I saved every card she ever sent me. The time she spent creating these love offerings made her feel vital, useful, connected, and engaged. It always made me feel special to be the recipient.

When I visited her assisted-living home, we would often go to the craft room together. I recall one time when we were making something using Popsicle sticks and beads. The sweetest woman was sitting next to my mom. I can't recall her name, but Mom knew her well. She was a resident on the same floor, and like my mom, her disabilities were more physical than emotional or mental. On this particular day, her daughter, who was also visiting, was sitting next to her.

As this precious elderly woman was stringing beads, I watched her get so excited about creating this little project. She was really having fun. At the same time, I watched her daughter get more and more agitated, clearly impatient with the slow progress her mother was making. Suddenly, she literally grabbed the project from her mother's hand and said, "Here, let me help you," and proceeded to quickly string the beads.

It was so sad. The light went out of her mother's face. I watched as her joy was robbed and her excitement just died. Far from helping, this daughter's response was handicapping. It was cruel.

I would like to think she wasn't intentionally being malicious, that in her heart she really did think she was helping. But her tone of voice, impatience, and rude behavior was hurtful.

When we overstep other people's boundaries, they often don't know how to tell us. They may fear losing us as much as we fear losing them.

We Enable Because...

The dynamic of enabling has many components. Our actions and behavior may be hurting instead of helping because...

- We have confused helping with enabling.
- We love too much, too little, too dependently, or too conditionally.
- We fear for our loved one's safety, the consequences, or the unknown.
- We feel guilty.
- We have never dealt with our own painful past issues, including abandonment, abuse, addictions, and a host of painful circumstances that have shaped us.

- Our personality traits make us prone to enable.
- What we're doing is all we know to do.
- Keeping the status quo is sometimes easier than changing.
- We think what we're doing is the right thing to do as Christians.
- We make excuses because drugs and alcohol have disabled or handicapped our loved ones.
- We are ignorant and don't know any better.
- We haven't stopped long enough to hear the still, small Voice of the Spirit and pray for SANITY.

Are You an Enabling Mother?

If your boundary issues involve an adult child, here are a few questions that might help determine the difference between helping and enabling. Alcoholics Anonymous uses similar questions when discussing living with an alcoholic or drug addict.

1. Have you loaned him money repeatedly without being repaid?
2. Have you paid for education or job training in more than one field?
3. Have you finished a job or project that he failed to complete himself because it was easier than arguing with him?
4. Have you paid his bills?
5. Have you accepted part of the blame for his addictions or behavior?

6. Have you avoided talking about negative issues because you feared his response?

7. Have you bailed him out of jail or paid his legal fees?

8. Have you given him one more chance—and then another and another?

9. Have you ever returned home or called at lunchtime and found him still in bed sleeping?

10. Have you wondered how he gets money to buy cigarettes, video games, new clothes, and such but can't afford to pay his own bills?

11. Have you ever "called in sick" for your child, lying about his symptoms to his boss?

12. Have you threatened to throw him out without following through?

13. Have you begun to feel that you've reached the end of your rope?

14. Have you begun to hate both your child and yourself for the way you live?

15. Have you begun to worry that the financial burden is more than you can bear?

16. Is your marriage in jeopardy because of this situation?

17. Are other family members becoming resentful because of this issue?

18. Are other people uncomfortable around you when this issue arises?

19. Have profanity, violence, or other unacceptable behavior become more common?

20. Are things missing from your home, such as money, valuables, and other personal property?

If you answered yes to several of these questions, you have probably enabled your adult child to avoid his own responsibilities—to escape the consequences of his actions. Rather than help your child grow into a productive and responsible adult, you have made it easier for him to get worse. Your enabling has probably contributed to the growing and continuing problem.

It's time to stop.

Is It Really Our Responsibility?

Unfortunately, many women are approaching critical stages of burnout because they're living multiple lives—their own, their children's, their spouses', their coworkers', their friends', their aging parents'...and the list goes on. Meanwhile, these women are saying, "But I'm only trying to help."

We must understand that in many instances, our helping is hurting. We must come to understand what our responsibility *is* and what it *isn't*.

Henry Cloud and John Townsend, authors of *Boundaries: When to Say Yes, When to Say No to Take Control of Your Life*, offer this explanation.

> Made in the image of God, we were created to take responsibility for certain tasks. Part of taking responsibility, or ownership, is knowing what *is* our job, and what *isn't*. Workers who continually take on duties that aren't theirs will eventually burn out. It takes wisdom to know what we should be doing and what we shouldn't. We can't do everything. [1]

Wisdom isn't something we suddenly attain, like fast food. "I'll take one order of wisdom to go, please." Wisdom comes from accumulated knowledge, insight, and judgment—it takes time to acquire. It also comes from God. The Bible says, "The LORD gives wisdom; from his mouth come knowledge and understanding" (Proverbs 2:6).

Consistently applying the Six Steps to SANITY can help to increase your wisdom.

As we conclude this chapter, take a serious look at areas of your life where you might have become an enabler. If none exist, so much the better. But if you see yourself as an enabler, consider establishing boundaries with the person you've been enabling. Write down some boundaries for yourself in your notebook. Enabling is negative behavior, and remember, your first SANITY Step is to *Stop Your Own Negative Behavior*.

Taking Control

1. Do you think you may naturally be prone to enabling others?

2. Who are you enabling now or in danger of enabling in the future?

3. Are you prepared to put in place a protective or restorative boundary with the person you're enabling and a preventative boundary with the person you can see yourself enabling in the future?

4

Your Most Important Boundary

Above all else, guard your heart, for everything you do flows from it"
(Proverbs 4:23).

I've mentioned several important areas of life where women usually need to set boundaries, including relationships, home, workplace,
church, and self. We've distinguished between helping and enabling,
but I've deliberately set aside the most critical difference for this chapter. It's that important.

Before a woman makes relational and psychological boundaries,
she must consider her most necessary boundary—that of guarding
her own heart. By that I mean a woman should know and respect the
boundaries God has given for her heart's protection. Protection is, after
all, one of the purposes of boundaries.

According to Scripture, everything we do flows from our heart.
Therefore, once this primary boundary is in place, we can set all other
boundaries much more easily.

How We Guard Our Hearts

We guard our hearts most effectively by knowing God's Word and
applying it to our lives personally. We keep God's Word buried deep

within us. With the Word we are able to defeat our enemies, overcome our fears, and remain confident women in the face of opposition.

Jesus Himself is our example. When Satan tempted Jesus in the wilderness, Jesus spoke the Word of God to refute everything Satan said. In doing this, Jesus told him that we live by "every word that comes from the mouth of God" (Matthew 4:4).

Just as Jesus was tempted, so too are we. The enemy knows our every weakness, and he will use his strategies to exploit those weaknesses. But even with his entire arsenal aimed at us, Satan can't prevail against God's Word. It's our most powerful tool of protection.

So think of God's Word as a boundary you must set in place in your heart. It's a preventive, protective, and restorative boundary, all at the same time.

God's Word is available to every Christian who will use it. God is for us in our every battle. He's with us in our decision to set boundaries. He tells us, "Do not fear, for I am with you; do not be dismayed, for I am your God. I will strengthen you and help you; I will uphold you with my righteous hand" (Isaiah 41:10).

God used Proverbs 4:23, the verse opening this chapter, to change my life when my adult son's choices were breaking my heart. This Scripture set me on a course to gain the strength I needed to make tough-love choices in my relationship with him and more fully develop my personal relationship with the Lord.

It led me on a journey to escape the bondage that chronic enabling brings, which eventually led me to develop the Six Steps to SANITY and write *Setting Boundaries® with Your Adult Children*, the first book in the Setting Boundaries® series. God continues to use the core message of this Scripture to mold me into the person He wants me to be.

Guarding our hearts isn't a one-time action. It requires a lifelong commitment. It's a permanent boundary, not a temporary one. To illustrate this nugget of life-changing wisdom, let's look at that same verse from several Bible versions.

- "Watch over your heart with all diligence, for from it flow the springs of life" (NASB).
- "Keep vigilant watch over your heart; that's where life starts" (MSG).
- "Keep and guard your heart with all vigilance and above all that you guard, for out of it flow the springs of life" (AMP).
- "Keep thy heart with all diligence; for out of it are the issues of life" (KJV).
- "Guard your heart above all else, for it determines the course of your life" (NLT).

The wording in the NLT has powerful implications. Think about it. When something determines the course of our life, it's pretty significant. The KJV aptly sums it up, for out of your heart are the issues of life. The translations all share the same basic truth—if we don't protect our hearts, we are in for a world of hurt, and so is everyone in our path.

Preparing the Heart

The first thing in all of life is to know God and enjoy Him. Acknowledging and knowing God helps us to become what we were meant to be. King David gave this counsel to his son.

> As for you, my son Solomon, know the God of your father, and serve Him with a loyal heart and with a willing mind; for the LORD searches all hearts and understands all the intent of the thoughts. If you seek Him, He will be found by you; but if you forsake Him, He will cast you off forever (1 Chronicles 28:9 NKJV).

As we prepare and guard our hearts and serve God with loyal hearts, He will protect our hearts and love us unconditionally. His love will help us gain power and purpose in life.

Repairing the Heart

In my journey to understand the significance of setting healthy boundaries, I learned that I would never enjoy true change in my relationships until I took responsibility for my own heart. I needed to stop my own negative behavior and understand my own motivations and emotions. God impressed on me that I needed to repair my own heart in accordance with His will and teaching, and only then would I find the hope, peace, and knowledge to make the difficult choices and changes I needed to make.

Remember what the Bible says in Isaiah 41:10: "Do not fear, for I am with you." As Christians, the only thing we need to fear is a heart that doesn't fear the Lord—a heart that is unprotected against the onslaught of a sinful nature and a sinful world.

> You must fear the LORD your God and worship him and cling to him. Your oaths must be in his name alone. He alone is your God, the only one who is worthy of your praise, the one who has done these mighty miracles that you have seen with your own eyes (Deuteronomy 10:20-21 NLT).

We begin to fear the Lord by obeying the call to guard our hearts and surrender them to Him. It's up to us to take the first step. It's up to us to exert the control God has granted us and willingly ask Him to help us prepare our hearts and repair.

Healthy Boundaries, Healthy Heart

Those of us who are boundary-challenged are often so caught up in drama, chaos, and crisis (caused

Those of us who are boundary-challenged are often so caught up in drama, chaos, and crisis (caused by our unclear or violated boundaries) that we neglect to obey God. When we don't intentionally walk in the spiritual authority God has given us, feelings of guilt, rejection, insecurity, anger, and fear consume us. These often make it difficult to hear His voice.

by our unclear or violated boundaries) that we neglect to obey God. When we don't intentionally walk in the spiritual authority God has given us, feelings of guilt, rejection, insecurity, anger, and fear consume us. These often keep us from hearing His voice.

In fact, many of us are so busy being good Christian women—making sacrifices, turning the other cheek, and taking care of other people, other issues, and other priorities—that we've ignored God's call to guard and protect our own hearts first. "Above all else, guard your heart, for everything you do flows from it" (Proverbs 4:23).

I began my journey with the Lord at age 35. I was a tangled-up mess of emotions when I asked Him to redeem, prepare, repair, and radically change my heart. I prayed, "Jesus, I've been going down the wrong road, and I want to make a U-turn toward You. Please forgive my sins and come into my life. Fill me with Your love and the power of the Holy Spirit. Heal my broken heart."

Regardless of whether you have prayed a similar prayer, if you feel that you are heading in the wrong direction, apply the "S" Step in SANITY—*Stop Your Own Negative Behavior*—and make a U-turn now. Ask God to be the Navigator of your life. If you have never asked the Lord into your heart, I invite you to do so now by repeating my U-turn prayer above. Let God prepare, repair, and change your heart.

The Bible says, "Don't worry about anything; instead, pray about everything. Tell God what you need, and thank him for all he has done. This is how we experience God's peace, which exceeds anything we can understand. His peace will guard your hearts and minds as you live in Christ Jesus" (Philippians 4:6-7 NLT).

As you begin to discover the way your weak or nonexistent boundaries may be contributing to a lack of peace, ask the Holy Spirit to guard your heart, to reveal what it is you need to stop, and to give you the strength to do it.

The Start to Healing Your Heart

Let's look at a woman who needed a boundary to guard her heart.

Margaret is a good wife, mother, and employee. She volunteers in the nursery at church every Sunday. She is dependable and conscientious, and she wants to please God and others. Unfortunately, people tend to take advantage of her goodwill.

Margaret has trouble speaking up or asking for help, and lately she's begun to feel exhausted, unsupported, and depressed. When her teenage son treats her disrespectfully, her husband laughs it off, and neither of them will help around the house. Recently, instead of confronting a fellow volunteer at church who wasn't fulfilling her responsibilities, Margaret picked up the slack herself.

At her job, Margaret sits by a rude coworker—an office bully who often leaves her in tears by the end of the day. She juggles all her responsibilities and those of others like a quiet soldier day in and day out.

To make matters worse, Margaret discovered her husband was having an affair the same night she discovered her teenage son had stolen her debit card, withdrawn $500 from her checking account, and had been arrested for drunk driving.

Her already overburdened and unprotected heart was now thoroughly broken.

Margaret's story reminds me of an experience I had one day, when I noticed a repetitive theme in two TV programs I had watched.

First, a poignant episode of *Touched By an Angel* featured an alcoholic mother faced with difficult choices when confronted by her adult daughter in a tough-love intervention. Then, in an unsettling episode of *Dr. Phil* titled "Teenage Rage," two parents shared their fear of being murdered by their only child.

Two entirely different programs with similar core truths. Hearts were being broken, and drastic consequences were imminent if new boundaries weren't established immediately. Both situations called for radical change.

That was Margaret's situation. She had to make radical changes. She had to learn to set healthy boundaries. But how does a compliant woman like Margaret find the strength and wisdom to make choices that will change her life? Where does she start?

She starts with her own heart. There she will find the fortitude to make choices that will change the story of her life.

In her desire to be everything to everybody even when she was treated poorly, Margaret had stopped hearing God's voice. In fact, she had stopped communicating with Him altogether. No one respected her anymore, including herself.

When the bottom fell out of Margaret's life, she was faced with critical choices. She could continue to make passive and unhealthy choices that left her heart unprotected, or she could take control and do something entirely different, something proactive.

The key to effectively setting boundaries is to do so rationally and not emotionally, with firmness and love, from an authentic place of truth and maturity. However, that is sometimes easier said than done, especially during times of trial. Still, God can always make a way when there seems to be no way, especially when we intentionally pray for wisdom and discernment.

And that is exactly what Margaret did. She was overwhelmed by her emotions and by the decisions she needed to make. She didn't know what her next steps should be. But God was preparing her heart for change.

She said, "My first inclination was to rush to the bank and take out a loan on the house to bail my son out of jail. Thankfully, I had recently learned the SANITY Steps, and when I stopped long enough to be still and pray about it, the Voice of the Spirit was loud and clear in my heart. It was time for me to stop my usual responses. I needed help developing a different plan of action."

Fortunately for Margaret, she was in a SANITY Support Group at her church. She realized she needed to apply the "A" Step in SANITY: *Assemble Supportive People.* Within a few hours, a small group of trusted men and women were sitting at her dining room table, praying with her and confidentially discussing her options and the steps she could take. Ultimately, the decision would be hers to make, but having input from these objective people helped Margaret develop an action plan and get through a time when painful emotions could have crippled her.

God began the process of repairing her heart.

In order to find SANITY, Margaret had to accept the part she had played in the dysfunctional dynamic. She also had to take action—she needed to change her perspective on control.

By doing so, she was able to weather the storm of her son's incarceration, the pain of an eventual divorce, and the uncertainty of a life she had never anticipated.

"At this point, I'm not sure what God has planned for me," she says. "But the more I learn about His nature and His will for my life, the more I trust in His unfailing love and protection."

Taking Control

1. In what areas do you need to guard your heart?

2. Begin to put the protective boundary of God's Word around your heart by reading Psalm 91 below.

> Whoever dwells in the shelter of the Most High
>   will rest in the shadow of the Almighty.
> I will say of the Lord, "He is my refuge and my fortress,
>   my God, in whom I trust."
> Surely he will save you
>   from the fowler's snare
>   and from the deadly pestilence.
> He will cover you with his feathers,
>   and under his wings you will find refuge;
>   his faithfulness will be your shield and rampart.
> You will not fear the terror of night,
>   nor the arrow that flies by day,
> nor the pestilence that stalks in the darkness,
>   nor the plague that destroys at midday.
> A thousand may fall at your side,
>   ten thousand at your right hand,
>   but it will not come near you.

You will only observe with your eyes
  and see the punishment of the wicked.
If you say, "The LORD is my refuge,"
  and you make the Most High your dwelling,
no harm will overtake you,
  no disaster will come near your tent.
For he will command his angels concerning you
  to guard you in all your ways;
they will lift you up in their hands,
  so that you will not strike your foot against a stone.
You will tread on the lion and the cobra;
  you will trample the great lion and the serpent.
"Because he loves me," says the LORD, "I will rescue him;
  I will protect him, for he acknowledges my name.
He will call on me, and I will answer him;
  I will be with him in trouble,
  I will deliver him and honor him.
With long life I will satisfy him
  and show him my salvation."

3. Close the book for a few minutes and simply open your
   heart to God. Tell Him all that's troubling you. Lean hard
   on Him. Ask Him to shine a light on the steps you need to
   take next.

5

Why Setting Boundaries
Is So Difficult for Christian Women

As part of the research for every book in the Setting Boundaries® series, I distribute a lengthy questionnaire in order to receive broader insight from others. In the survey for this book, I asked, "Why do you think some women have more trouble than others when it comes to understanding and setting healthy boundaries?"

Many responded that the way we interpret the Bible plays an important role. One person replied, "Women frequently misinterpret what the Bible is saying."

This is really no surprise. Many sources influence and shape the way we understand the Bible.

The late Catherine Clark Kroeger held a PhD from the University of Minnesota. She was adjunct associate professor of classical and ministry studies at Gordon-Conwell Theological Seminary and co-editor (with James Beck) of *Women, Abuse, and the Bible* and *Healing the Hurting*. Mary J. Evans teaches Old Testament at London Bible College and is the author of *Woman in the Bible* and *1 and 2 Samuel* in the *New International Bible Commentary*.

Together, these dynamic and gifted women created *The IVP Women's Bible Commentary*. They write…

> Every reader of the Bible is also an interpreter of it, but all interpretations are invariably influenced by sources other than Scripture. Cultural, ethnic, social, gender and economic experiences factor into the interpreter's perspective and thus shape how a reader might understand a text.[1]

How we understand and interpret the Bible is inextricably linked to the way we apply its message.

Consider a woman who interprets the Bible as an ancient document that depicts most women as second-class citizens and justifies control of women through abuse and subjugation. She sees herself as a victim who has no control. Her application of the biblical message is that she deserves to be treated poorly because she is a woman and this is her lot in life. Therefore, she believes she must learn to accept her feelings of inadequacy and unworthiness. She must be content to please those who control her destiny.

This example may appear extreme, but it demonstrates the link between interpretation and application.

If we see the Samaritan woman at the well as a pathetic victim of cruel men and poor choices, we may conclude that we too are victims. But if we see her life as an empowering example of the Lord's restoration and redemption, we are much more likely to embrace the unconditional love and freedom He extended to her and now extends to us.

Licensed Christian counselor Dawn Irons provided this insightful response to the questionnaire.

> I think women, especially Christian women, have been conditioned by well-meaning people who have taken Scripture out of context to reduce a woman's role in the home, society, and church as one of only service and hospitality. Granted, many women are wired with a heart and desire to bless people with those genuine spiritual gifts, but

if we're not careful, a form of legalistic spiritual abuse can cause women to be run over roughshod with demands and expectations. They are taught that to be a good Christian woman, they must do good. Many women have difficulty saying no to requests from the church to serve here or there. Other women have trouble saying no to their children because they have been conditioned to believe that there is somehow a conflict between being nurturing and being a disciplinarian. We are called to *do* and *be* both—but many women feel guilty if they are not living up to the cruel fairy tale of "supermom" or the biblical example of the very intimidating Mrs. Proverbs 31.

The Roots of Bible Interpretation

Before I made my U-turn toward God, I was perplexed because Christianity appeared to oppose any kind of female strength. It seemed to me the focus for women was primarily on submission and subservience, and I felt that if I embraced this belief system, I would lose my individual identity, sense of self, and personal power.

I've come to believe this is a very clever lie the enemy has used as a stronghold to convince women not to follow Jesus. To render women as ineffective as possible and convince us that Christianity is all about being controlled by others, being submissive, and losing our sense of identity—which couldn't be further from the truth. A deep devotion to Jesus does not mean a loss of self. It means we find ourselves.

Some Jewish rabbis taught that a man should not speak to a woman in public, but Jesus not only spoke to a Samaritan woman in public but also drank from her cup (John 4:1-30). The first person He appeared to after His resurrection was Mary Magdalene (John 20:11-18). Clearly, Jesus had a very high view of women. God's Word tells us, "There is neither Jew nor Gentile, neither slave nor free, nor is there male and female, for you are all one in Christ Jesus" (Galatians 3:28).

I didn't start reading the Bible until I was 35, and only after another decade could I approach it with an open heart. My exposure before that was when as kids, my younger brother and I would page through our huge King James Version of the Holy Bible. It included glossy full-page color illustrations of classical works of art that often showed scantily clad women and men—very racy stuff. Mom had purchased our Bible on one of our trips to the Goodwill Thrift Store. Something about it must have spoken to her, although I have no recollection of seeing her open it. For the most part (I'm sorry to say now), this huge tome was often used either as a doorstop or as a weight to press our colorful autumn leaves after we ironed them between sheets of waxed paper.

How thankful I am today that I appreciate and understand the Bible as far more than a paperweight.

My lack of respect and appreciation for the Bible as a child wasn't so much irreverence as it was ignorance. A plaque of the Ten Commandments hung from the kitchen wall in my childhood home, but we weren't a churchgoing family. My mom loved to read and encouraged us to do so as well, but the Bible wasn't important in her life. Mom was a strong woman of moral character and values, but she wasn't a vocal proponent of organized religion. Unfortunately, she equated the Bible with the church. She didn't go to church, so she didn't read the Bible. I think her reticence to get involved in church had a lot to do with her divorce, which wasn't socially acceptable when I was a child. I believe Mom felt ostracized in many social situations, including the church. Thinking about that makes me sad today.

However, I do remember being picked up by a small bus and attending a vacation Bible school at a local church during summer vacations. This is where I learned familiar Bible stories, watched flannel-board presentations, and tried (unsuccessfully) to memorize Scripture in order to win prizes.

It was also where my young inquisitive mind questioned my value as a female in the eyes of God. Every story prominently featured men—Jonah and the whale, Noah and his ark, David and Goliath, Joseph and his coat of many colors, and of course, Moses and his commandments. In fact, from my perspective, the only person who seemed to have anything whatsoever to do with women was Jesus, and I based that opinion on a large framed picture in the church basement. Jesus was sitting on a rock in a field with a group of little boys and girls gathered at His feet.

Overall, it appeared to me that women weren't very important in the Bible, a fact that made it hard for me to embrace its relevance in my life. I couldn't relate to the Bible then, making it all the more difficult to relate to it decades later as an adult believer.

A Catastrophic Change

The truth is, Christ valued women, and they played an important role in His ministry, as Scripture clearly indicates. Yet the power and influence of women was gradually suppressed as Scripture was interpreted more and more out of context. Faith Martin writes about this in her book *Call Me Blessed: The Emerging Christian Woman.*

> The early Christian fathers had little difficulty removing women from the authority structure of the church because they believed that women were spiritually inferior to men. Because the woman was created from the man, they believed that it was man's image that woman reflected, not God's. This was combined with the teaching that woman was "fleshly" and inclined to evil; being the first to sin in Eden, woman proved her fundamental spiritual weakness.

> The reasoning of the early fathers is easy enough to follow, but what is hard to understand is how such teaching could develop so quickly after the ministry of Jesus and the example set by Paul. The Gospels and the book of Acts are filled with the activity of women. The inspired writings contain hearty commendation of not only the faith of the women but their *work* on behalf of Christ. Paul closes his letter to the Romans with personal greetings to twenty-eight saints for whom he has special commendation. Ten of them are women.

Under Paul, women of means opened their homes for
church meetings and, it is generally acknowledged, led
the congregations that met in their homes; by the time
the buildings were erected for the purpose of worship,
women entered by a side door and sat behind a partition.
This change began at the end of the first century when the
inspired writings ceased and the doctrine of the spiritual
inferiority of women began to be introduced.[2]

Unfortunately, the doctrine of spiritual inferiority began and
flourished as a result of an incorrect interpretation of Scripture. It was
developed and passed down through generations in opinions, lectures,
sermons, doctrinal creeds, and Bible commentary.

No wonder Christian women sometimes struggle to set healthy
boundaries in life. Many women remain confused about their role in the
church, doubt their own value, or question their identity in God's eyes.

The Sanity of the Gospel Message

Although men and women
most assuredly possess different
gifts, strengths, and roles, women
are no less valued by God and certainly not spiritually inferior. Our
Almighty Creator has designed us
for a purpose. The Bible says, "We
are God's masterpiece. He has created us anew in Christ Jesus, so
we can do the good things he
planned for us long ago" (Ephesians 2:10 NLT).

The biblical text that shapes and
empowers everyone is
characterized by the central gospel
message that Christ came to
redeem all people through the
cross, call them into a life of
discipleship, and create a
community of faith as the physical
presence of God's work in the
world.

The biblical text that shapes and empowers everyone is characterized by the central gospel message that Christ came to redeem all
people through the cross, call them into a life of discipleship, and create a community of faith as the physical presence of God's work in

the world. The Bible says, "I am writing to you who are God's children because your sins have been forgiven through Jesus. I am writing to you who are mature in the faith because you know Christ, who existed from the beginning. I am writing to you who are young in the faith because you have won your battle with the evil one" (1 John 2:12-13 NLT).

All Christians would agree that we need to submit to God's authority, that we're accountable to God first and to human authority second, but there is ongoing disagreement about the way we are to do that—especially as women.

In the Christian community, the subject of women's equality has long been a source of dissension. It's not my intention to argue theological belief systems or in any way to infer that one denominational position is right and another is wrong.

> We can be strong women of faith who uphold Christian family values while at the same time understand that God does not diminish our worth as women—that He loves His daughters just as much as He loves His sons.

However, God impresses on my heart time and again that we can be strong women of faith who uphold Christian family values while at the same time understand that God does not diminish our worth as women—that He loves His daughters just as much as He loves His sons.

Jesus died for the sins of both women and men, and the whole of the Bible is for both men and women, and the perspectives of both need to be considered and valued by all in order for all of God's children to live powerful and productive lives for the Lord. We women can and must expect God to use us as fully as He uses men. And we must expect that He speaks to us just as often and as clearly as He does to men.

Authors Henry T. Blackaby and Claude V. King write, "God speaks to individuals, and He can do it in any way He pleases. As you walk in an intimate love relationship with God, you will come to recognize His voice. You will know when God is speaking to you. He will see to it."[3]

How does God speak to you? Do you interpret Him through a lens of loving acceptance or legalistic dogma? Are you walking in the freedom of salvation and in the possibilities of purpose? Have you claimed the spiritual authority God has given you? Or are you straining against the bonds of oppression and the unrealistic expectations of others?

My point, of course, is that if you've been taken advantage of because you're a woman, and you've come to accept that treatment as something God designed for you as a second-class citizen, that wrong perception must change. As author and speaker Karen O'Connor says, "We are by nature nurturers and caregivers and seem to be born with the instinct to think of others before ourselves, but in the process some of us abandon the person we were designed to be."

A surefire way to get in touch with who we were designed to be is to learn more about God's ultimate plan and purpose for our lives, as outlined in His divinely inspired Word—the Holy Bible.

6

Encountering God's Word and Wisdom

Every Christian woman who desires to feel the power of God's gracious and generous love must consider the way she encounters and embraces the wisdom of His Word. Regardless of how much or how little biblical knowledge we have, we can connect with God's Word and allow it to change us from the inside out and make a positive impact in the world around us.

Whether we're seeking a more intimate relationship with the Lord, looking for a deeper understanding of our life, or confronting challenging relationships or circumstances, so much depends on learning what God wants to teach us through Scripture.

standing of our life, or confronting challenging relationships or circumstances, so much depends on learning what God wants to teach us through Scripture.

The world of Christian publishing has grown considerably since I wrote my first book in 2001. Today, a wealth of material addresses the hunger many women have to experience and interpret Scripture in a fresh and relevant way, including numerous Bible commentaries and studies.

However, the most important resource is the Bible itself.

Before 1881, you could read any version of the Bible you wanted—as long as it was the King James Version. Today, numerous translations of the Bible enable us to read, compare, and interpret Scripture in various styles. Each translation has the power to transform our lives. The cadence and terminology may differ, but the voice of God can speak to us through each one.

Regardless of what version of the Bible you prefer, these are key questions: How will you respond to God's voice as He speaks to you from the pages of this life-changing book? Will you allow the Holy Spirit to change your thinking, your responses, and your choices? Will you actively claim the gift of spiritual authority God has given you?

Divine Design

If we could paint a picture of who God designed us to be, we would paint Christ, wouldn't we? All of us—men and women—are designed to be Christlike. We women are all daughters of a great King, created in His image and called to be like Jesus. "God knew his people in advance, and he chose them to become like his Son, so that his Son would be the firstborn among many brothers and sisters" (Romans 8:29 NLT).

If we are like His Son, our character will reflect the character of Christ.

Unlike my childhood home, my house now has several Bibles. However, all the incredible wis-

> Having the Bible on my nightstand isn't the same as hiding His Word in my heart.

dom and guidance contained within their pages won't miraculously transport itself into my head and heart by osmosis. Having the Bible on my nightstand isn't the same as hiding His Word in my heart.

We must begin to read, interpret, and apply Scripture in ways that honor God and allow us to grow into fruitful women. We must learn what it means to walk in God's will. Ultimately, this is how we can learn to set healthy boundaries, find SANITY, and discover peace.

A Refreshing Resource

In my desire to encounter God's Word in ways that speak to contemporary women today, I've discovered a Bible commentary written and edited by two evangelical female scholars who are qualified to interpret Scripture from their own stance. This is an important resource that affirms the significance, power, and essential dignity of women in all aspects of life. It has helped me to understand and apply Scripture lessons with fresh perspective.

Catherine Clark Kroeger and Mary J. Evans write…

> Women need the opportunity to have the Scriptures explained in ways that are relevant to their lives. The Old Testament bears witness to the importance of the Scriptures being read and interpreted to all God's people (Deut 31:12; Josh 8:34-35; cf. 2 Kings 23:2). Just as Ezra made sure the Word was not only read but also interpreted for both men and women (Neh 8:1-8), so today the Scriptures need to be read and interpreted for women. But all too often, the interpretive voices of women have been lacking…

> The majority of commentaries available to today's readers of Scripture are written from the perspective of white, Western, classically educated, middle-class males, and the questions asked and issues raised are almost always dealt with from that perspective. Usually the work is done with integrity, insight and good scholarship, and the usefulness of the commentaries is by no means limited to those who share the same background as the writers. The answers found in Scripture to questions asked by men often bear great relevance to women; their insights are likely to be genuine insights into what Scripture is saying. Nevertheless, inevitable limitations arise from their curtailed perspective. Many insights into the text are never revealed simply because the

questions that might have revealed them have never been asked.[1]

What questions are you asking God as you study His Word? Undoubtedly, our questions will change as our lives change. Our interpretation of what God's Word is teaching us and what the Holy Spirit is revealing to us will most assuredly change as well. This is good as long as we continue to respond to His voice and allow Him to speak to us through the pages of this life-changing book.

Women Who Changed Their World

I've grown much closer to the Lord over the years by studying the lives of women in the Bible as they relate to contemporary women.

> Prominent in Old Testament history was the judge Deborah. Judges 4:4 tells us, "Deborah, a prophetess, the wife of Lappidoth, was leading Israel at that time." Judges 5:7 also tells us that she was a mother. This competent woman was not only a spiritual and governmental leader, but she was the inspiration behind Barak's military expedition against Sisera. She delivered the word of the Lord to Barak and then, at his express request, accompanied him on the campaign. The text of Judges 4 and 5 shows that she was the dominant figure of this era, but more interesting, the account is given in a very straightforward manner. The Scripture includes no disclaimer to the effect that the Lord could not find any man willing to lead Israel, so he was forced to settle for a woman. Clearly, not only was Deborah a multitalented individual whose qualities made her readily accepted by the people as their prophet and judge, she also used her gifts of encouragement and exhortation as she helped Barak move out to obey God's command.[2]

Deborah is only one of the prominent women in the Bible who played a significant role in history. It's impossible to mention all the important women of the Bible, including Sarah, Hagar, Hannah, Ruth and Naomi, Martha and Mary, and Mary the mother of Jesus. Hundreds of other not-so-familiar women listed in the Bible include those who had an active role in the story of God's relationship with His people as well as women named in genealogies, greeted in letters, or mentioned in passing.

The women whose lives are revealed in the ancient stories of love and loss, mistakes and mercy, and fear and faith can offer valuable lessons for us today. I encourage you to spend time with these women in a fresh new way. Ask God to shine a new light of inspiration, interpretation, and knowledge on your heart, to equip and empower you with the truth that not only sets us free but also enables us to become the women God wants us to be.

The world is rapidly changing in fascinating and frightening ways. As we study God's Word and apply these divinely inspired teachings to our lives, we are taking responsibility for the call to protect our hearts and put God first—a call that will prepare us for whatever the future might bring.

Quite simply, I believe God is equipping His warrior women to do great things in the world. He is restoring hearts and souls and redirecting and preparing us to make a difference in our families, churches, communities, and yes, even in our world.

We need more Deborah disciples—competent and courageous women who love the Lord with passion and purpose. Women who are able to set healthy boundaries and, with God's help, change their lives.

When Boundaries Are Violated

Some people say the issue of women in ministry is more divisive than any other that has confronted the church since the Reformation. However, while women's roles continue to be debated and opposing positions declared, another controversial issue in Christendom has faced believers since long before Martin Luther published his *Ninety-Five Theses* in 1517. The issue of excessive control—the abuse and subjugation of women—has proven to be a powerful stronghold of the enemy.

The mistaken notion that women are second-class citizens is bad enough, but even worse, some women are subjected to abuse because of that low status. Abuse can occur when a man feels he has the right to subjugate the woman in his life or when a woman doesn't take action to stand against such subjugation.

My dictionary lists these synonyms of "subjugate": conquer, subdue, enslave, reduce, overcome, overthrow, vanquish, defeat, and beat. All are powerful words when referring to warfare but quite disconcerting when used to describe the treatment of women.

Many women have never experienced the trauma of physical or sexual abuse. But dozens of studies spanning a wide variety of situations and subjects lead us to believe there are far more of us who have.

Over the years, I've searched the Bible to find meaning from the experiences in my life, particularly those where my boundaries were severely violated. I have cried out to God, "What exactly do You want me to do with these experiences, God? What purpose can these possibly serve? What am I supposed to learn from all of this?" And while the lessons have been many, I'm frequently prompted to ponder God's gift of free will.

We know that God protects and loves all of His children. However, He has given us the gift of free will, or free choice. Therefore, though God protects and loves us, He also extends that gift of free will to people who use it to violate His commandments and inflict pain and suffering on others. Os Hillman explores this problem.

> God took a huge risk when He gave man free will. By giving man free will it meant that God would be blamed for many things that Satan would do. By giving man free will He knew that evil would work through man and man would blame God for the evil instead of Satan, who is the author of evil.[1]

This raises important questions, and the answers don't come easily. However, God wants to free us from oppression and heal both the abused and the abuser. Transformation can and does occur in abusive relationships. However, on the road to restoration in a relationship, the perpetrator must be held accountable—by himself, society, the church, and his spouse or loved one. Assault on one's partner is not merely a domestic dispute. It's a crime, and it should be treated as such.

> When we repeatedly accept the violation of our boundaries through abuse, the hurt can escalate to frightening proportions. Then resistance becomes much more dangerous.

I've participated in countless domestic-violence support groups over the years as a victim and a survivor, as both a speaker and an observer. I've heard many women say that things would have been different if they had been able to seriously and effectively object when the abusive treatment first started—that is, if they had gotten help sooner. When we repeatedly accept the violation of our boundaries through abuse, the hurt can escalate to frightening proportions. Then resistance becomes much more dangerous.

Years ago, when I was a newlywed and my husband first began to hit me, I couldn't wrap my brain around what was actually happening. At first, I blamed myself for making him angry, but as the violence escalated I began to think differently. I wasn't a believer at the time, so I didn't know that God's Word condemned this kind of mistreatment. I only knew that if I didn't escape from this abuse, this man's rage would kill me. And I wasn't ready to die.

Countless resources are available to help, but we first need to realize that we need help and that we deserve to get help. Authors Catherine Clark Kroeger and Nancy Nason-Clark have written an insightful book addressing the issue of violence against women from a biblical perspective.

> Sometimes the victim can be led to an understanding of herself as a person of worth with a right to respect and kindly treatment. Created by the Father, redeemed by the Son and empowered by the Holy Spirit, she can become more respectful of herself. She can realize that it is wrong for anyone to call her names, to humiliate her or to treat her disrespectfully. The victim can perceive that she did not cause the abuse or "make him do it." While direct confrontation of the abuser may be very unsafe, she can understand that mistreatment is condemned by the Word of God and that she need not be a helpless mass of jelly nor accept cruel injustice. Sometimes such quiet conviction starts to bring about altered conduct from the offender, but by no means can this be assumed.
>
> At times there has been a supposition that the wife can extricate herself if the situation becomes too difficult.

Many people assume that the woman is able to leave an abusive situation of her own volition, that it is actually her own responsibility. But many women are too traumatized to take that step. A director of a battered women's project recently noted, "Victims of domestic violence are in an altered state. Up seems down...It's also important to understand that if [someone] was a victim all these years, it's sort of like she's been brainwashed. You are in essence, a prisoner." [2]

A Long History

Sadly, the subjugation of women and the abuse of control has had a long-standing tradition in the historically patriarchal religious community.

The Austin Family Violence Diversion Network and the Tyler Family Preservation Project, both based in Texas, help abusive couples and families discover ways to handle conflict without physical violence. Batterers in these programs are challenged concerning their patriarchal sex-role beliefs. The programs strive to create change in many of the batterer's attitudes, including his religious belief.

> "The hardest men to counsel are the older, religious men. They are stubborn and they never stop referring to the Bible," says John Patrick, a counselor with the Family Preservation Project. The men in these programs who mention their religious beliefs typically appeal to the Bible to justify their use of violence. They often use the word *submit* concerning their wives' failure to bow to their demands. Some of the men said that their wives must submit to them in order to be submitting to God. These men used religion as a rationale to dominate women and to excuse occasional violence as necessary discipline. [3]

The Bible says, "An angry person stirs up conflict, and a hot-tempered person commits many sins" (Proverbs 29:22). The Bible also says we are to be controlled by the Spirit—not by man. "All who are led by the Spirit of God are children of God. So you have not received a spirit that makes you fearful slaves. Instead, you received God's Spirit when he adopted you as his own children" (Romans 8:14 -15 NLT).

Some men exercise control over women with physical abuse and violence, but countless men would never raise a hand to their loved one. Instead, they exercise their control with emotional, verbal, or spiritual abuse. I would like to believe in most cases this unhealthy control and violation of boundaries is not intentional. It could be a mirroring response based on learned behavior. It could also be a faulty belief system—a misinterpretation of the biblical teaching on submission.

> The idea that Christian women must tolerate suffering from abuse as a component of forgiveness is in no way biblical.

The biblical call for wives to submit to husbands was never intended to place women in positions of danger. Violated boundaries not only threaten our physical and emotional safety but also keep us in debilitating spiritual bondage. They keep us from living the lives God intended for us and from being the people God designed us to be.

The idea that Christian women must tolerate suffering from abuse as a component of forgiveness is in no way biblical. Authors Kroeger and Beck address this issue.

> Wives are often encouraged not to challenge their husband's authority, but to be covertly manipulative in order to influence his decision-making. Many Christian writers who address the issue of abuse usually begin by stating that the husband is responsible for his own abusive behavior. However, that statement is frequently negated by a shift of focus to the wife. This shift usually results in a lengthy discussion about a woman's proper attitude and behavior in a Christian marriage and the devastating results of her failure to adequately follow what the writer believes to be

the biblical model of marriage established at creation. Special emphasis is placed on biblical passages that emphasize a wife's submission to her husband, the obligation to forgive those who hurt us and to tolerate suffering, and prohibitions against divorce. The influence of church teaching in these four areas (submission, suffering, forgiveness, and divorce) served as the framework for a survey conducted on the reaction and response of Christian battered women. [4]

At no point in God's Word are women instructed to be unequivocally submissive to anyone who would demonstrate excessive or dangerous control over their lives. However, the willingness to accept unacceptable treatment may be deeply ingrained in some of us as a type of "survival response," as Patrick Carnes explains.

> Children are presented with what trauma researcher David Calof has described as the "universal bind." Do not see, hear, sense, feel or address what is real. Instead, accept what is unreal and proscribed in the interest of your survival. Disbelieve the obvious, and accept the improbable. The bind is that the child is presented with only two options: (1) be overwhelmed with terror and not able to function, or (2) distort reality to survive. Because of the bind, distorting reality becomes part of the "working model" eventually used in adult relationships. [5]

Are you hesitant or even fearful to say no to your spouse? Do you have difficulty determining whether you are experiencing abuse? Some women will distort the reality by diminishing the violence with dangerous excuses. "It was only a push." "It was only a slap. It's not like he beats me." "He really didn't mean to hurt me or the children."

Assess the Danger

Whether physical, emotional, verbal, or spiritual abuse is recent, occasional, or habitual, if it is part of your life today, it's time to take control and seek help. If someone has violated a physical boundary and you fear for your safety or the safety of someone you are responsible for (such as a child or an aging parent), you must take control and protect yourself and your loved ones. If necessary, seek the help of legal authorities and other professionals.

> If physical abuse is a component of your relationship, please be very careful. It's critical that you make choices about your next steps from a rational position, not an emotional one.

I understand this won't be easy. However, there is no excuse for physical violence, and you alone must set a boundary of zero tolerance of physical abuse.

The "N" Step in SANITY is imperative in addressing this destructive and dangerous situation. We must *Nip Excuses in the Bud*. There is no excuse for abuse.

However, if physical abuse is a component of your relationship, please be very careful. It's critical that you make choices about your next steps from a rational position, not an emotional one. Author June Hunt offers this advice:

> Violent outbursts can occur at any time and can escalate when a husband senses or is informed his wife is leaving. A wife who is wise will have prepared for the worst by having a safety plan for leaving. For a detailed list of strategies and legal system information, please contact Hope for the Heart toll-free at 1-800-488-HOPE (4673) or www.hope fortheheart.org. [6]

A sidebar in *The Women's Study Bible* titled "Violence, Abuse, and Oppression" includes this:

> Women, especially Christian women, can have difficulty determining what counts as violence, abuse, and oppression. It may be easier to recognize the victimization of others than to identify such problems within our circle and family. These difficulties in recognizing abuse come

honestly. The Christian belief system and Scriptures are often understood to teach unrestricted self-sacrifice, endless forgiveness, humility as a chief virtue, and sin as pride and self-will. While these can represent valid components of a Christian theology, an uncritical appropriation of them often blinds women to the violence in their lives and in the lives of those close to them. It can also stop women from following Christ in opposing such injustice...

Scripture identifies what it feels like to receive violence, abuse, and oppression. One feels abandoned, overpowered, reduced, foolish, and even insane. The victim becomes "broken spirited" and experiences affliction, suffering, and loss. One may often feel angry at God, be unable to keep God's precepts and despair of life. There are good reasons for these feelings—the abused have been abandoned, let down or used by others, often by the people closest to us.

The victim feels anguish: the pain of being sinned against to the point of powerlessness. Anguish needs to be marked out as different from personal wrongdoing or sin. Anguish happens when our healthy expectation for interpersonal interdependency is subverted. Someone has used us for his or her ends. The distinguishing experience from the victim's perspective is that she has been rendered helpless.

All people have trouble motivating their wills to turn toward God, but victims have an additional problem. The trauma of being victimized can paralyze or reduce the ability of the will to break free. The more powerful the abuse or the fewer the resources, the more deeply one is put in bondage to one's anguish. Once trapped, the will is weakened or paralyzed, and outside intervention is necessary to break the grip (e.g., Exodus 6:6).[7]

Never Hesitate to Seek Professional Help

Bernis Riley is a licensed professional counselor and a member of the American Association of Christian Counselors and the Christian

Counselors of Texas. She addresses the issue of excessive control and the misinterpretation of Scripture often in her private practice at Soul-Care Counseling.

> Abuse is a blatant violation of boundaries. It crosses all physical, mental, emotional, and psychological boundaries. But not only does abuse violate another person's boundaries, abuse causes a deep wounding of the soul. If left untreated, this wound becomes infected with anger, bitterness, resentment, fear, disappointment, and self-loathing. If you are a survivor of abuse, whether as a child or as an adult, counseling is recommended to help you find healing for your wounds of abuse.[8]

As someone who has survived early childhood abuse and extreme domestic violence, I'm now acutely aware of the need to protect my physical boundaries. However, it took years of poor choices and painful experiences to understand how those violated boundaries affected virtually every aspect of my life—even years later.

My relationship with the Lord has brought healing and hope to my life, and domestic abuse hasn't played a part in my life for decades. But the effects have left lasting impressions. I know the damage this violation of boundaries can do to us.

I doubt I would be in the place I am today without the help and guidance I received from therapists and counselors over the years. If you're questioning your identity, self-worth, or value because of any type of violated boundaries in the past or present, I implore you to seek help from a licensed Christian counselor or a professional interventionist.

Sometimes life simply does not make sense. Our willingness to take control of our brokenness and seek help signals our desire to obey God and guard our hearts. The Bible says, "I am the LORD. I will free you from your oppression and will rescue you from your slavery in Egypt. I will redeem you with a powerful arm and great acts of judgment" (Exodus 6:6 NLT).

In addressing this issue, the "A" Step in SANITY is particularly helpful. Being objective in situations like this is often difficult, and that's okay. We don't have to go through it alone. In fact, God's Word instructs us that it isn't good to be alone—that it's important to depend on wise, godly counsel, especially in times of trial, tribulation, and uncertainty. Our willingness to *Assemble Supportive People* (and, when needed, professional people) can literally save our lives.

In a recent sermon message, Pastor Chuck Angel said, "Our capacity to exercise our spiritual authority increases when we get help and wise counsel from people who are anchored in the ancient timeless truth of God's Word, and we get stronger in conviction, confidence, and courage."

Dr. Laura Schlesinger offers this encouragement to assert proper control:

> The obvious question is, "What makes some people hold on to being a victim and others choose to improve their life?" The answer is control. When you are a perpetual victim, the past is in control of your present. When you are a conqueror, the present is controlled by your choices, in spite of the pain and the pull of your past.[9]

Remember, the Bible says, "In all these things we are more than conquerors through him who loved us" (Romans 8:37).

Regardless of the mistakes you have made in your life, you are not to blame if you are being abused. Remember, we cannot control the actions of others, but we can control our responses to them. We *can* learn how to say no. We *can* learn what the Word of God teaches us about the critical need to exercise kingdom authority. We *can* learn to claim that divine right and stand up against the enemy who uses abuse in our past or present to keep us from being the effective women of purpose, passion, and power God wants us to be.

Ask God to direct you to reliable advisors and sources of wisdom who can speak into your life, and then *Trust the Voice of the Spirit* (the

"T" Step in SANITY) to reveal how and when you should take control if physical violence is a reality in your life. Prepare to *Implement an Action Plan* (the "I" Step in SANITY) and make sure it includes a safety plan.

Proceed with caution and go with God.

Saying No Without Guilt

In addition to believing the lie that women are less than men, many women have grown accustomed to being automatically compliant when asked to take on projects or new relationships. Perhaps this is due to our natural desire to nurture. But whatever the reason, the result is often the same: Many women simply say yes to some things when they should say no.

The most basic boundary-setting word is "no." It lets others know that you exist apart from them and that you're in control of you. Being clear about your no and your yes is a theme that is echoed in the Bible. The following are two examples.

- "Just say a simple, 'Yes, I will,' or 'No, I won't.' Anything beyond this is from the evil one" (Matthew 5:37 NLT).

- "Most of all, my brothers and sisters, never take an oath, by heaven or earth or anything else. Just say a simple yes or no, so that you will not sin and be condemned" (James 5:12 NLT).

As natural-born nurturers, women have always had challenges saying no. This is often because we find it difficult to understand what is our responsibility and what isn't. We say yes to everything and try to do it all just to stay on the safe side. And because we simply can't do it all, we end up feeling guilty for that which we don't do. And if we're being truthful, sometimes we really don't want to do it all in the first place, but we erroneously think if we don't do it, no one else will.

That sense of guilt, combined with feelings of rejection, insecurity, embarrassment, and fear, keeps us from living fruitful lives. Negative feelings and behavior have perpetuated an epidemic of depression, enabling, and addiction among women. We must resist what I call the "silent killer"—the willingness to live on the exhausting gerbil wheel of insanity.

Perhaps we're asking the wrong question when we wonder why it's so difficult to say no. Instead, maybe we should be asking ourselves why we are saying yes in the first place. In some cases, we're too emotionally involved in a situation to consider it objectively. We often rely on our feelings rather than thinking matters through.

For example, I couldn't bear the thought of my son being in jail or addicted to drugs, so I did whatever I could to pay for bail and drug rehabilitation programs—until I realized my choices were hurting and not helping. Unfortunately, many of us make emotional choices in the heat of the moment, when we're faced with challenging situations, circumstances, or people.

In other cases, we say yes in order to fill a void in our lives and find meaning, value, purpose, or significance. We may volunteer to sit on another committee, take on another project, or cook another potluck dish.

Linda Evans Shepherd is an author, a speaker, and the founder of the Advanced Writers and Speakers Association. When I asked her about the challenges women have in saying no without guilt, this was her response.

> We all want to please our friends and loved ones, so we agree
> to do so many tasks that even Superwoman would be afraid
> of our to-do lists. But we have to remember, the person we

most need to please is God. When it comes to adding more
to our to-do lists, we must more closely follow the peace of
God instead of our own desire to please others.

The edict to say what you mean and mean what you say is a critical
component in any relationship, and it is especially critical here. When
we can master that skill, we'll be well on our way to a life with secure
boundaries. There is no excuse for someone's damaging, demeaning, or
dangerous behavior, but in some cases our own inability to set healthy
boundaries and follow through with appropriate consequences can
contribute to the way we're treated. People take their cues from us.
What message are we sending?

One of my favorite publications is *O, the Oprah Magazine.* I particularly like Oprah's monthly editorial, "What I Know for Sure." When
it comes to sending a clear message about setting boundaries, "what I
know for sure" is that there are three debilitating feelings that consistently come up when women have problems setting boundaries: guilt,
insecurity, and fear.

The Guise of Guilt

Guilty feelings corrode our emotional state. They are negative feelings that come when we judge ourselves as being wrong. Women carry
an enormous burden of guilt when they think, *What if…*or *If only I
had…*or *Why didn't I…*

Dawn Irons is a licensed professional counselor at SoulCare Counseling in Bedford, Texas. She talks with guilt-laden women frequently.
She wrote this in response to the questionnaire I distributed in research-
ing this book:

> Women have a bizarre guilt-switch that is often triggered
> when they sense they can't live up to everyone's expecta-
> tions. They continually compare themselves one to another,
> which will most often leave them feeling "less-than." So in
> one sense, saying no gives them a disadvantage in trying to
> keep up with the role of "Super-Mom/Wife." This problem

(and they need to realize this *is* a problem) creates situations where they have no concept that saying no can be the most healthy thing they can do. Saying no feels uncomfortable and wrong to them. This is a situation where boundary training and deep study of the Word of God can transform their minds and lives in a healthy way. But first, they need to recognize that, "Houston, we have a problem!"

Indeed we do. Setting healthy boundaries is all about choosing when to say yes, when to say no, when to say "Let me think about it," and when to say nothing at all. And once we make that choice, boundaries help us feel secure about it rather than feeling guilty.

We need not feel guilty for what we know in our heart and spirit is right.

Learning how to say no is difficult for many of us, especially for people pleasers. Our habits of response have locked many of us in a prison of our own making.

Additionally, when we begin to respond to others in a new way with firmness and love, it's equally important not to feel guilty about our new responses. Someone may try to lay a guilt trip on us, but we don't have to accept the ticket.

The Instability of Insecurity

The second debilitating feeling we have is insecurity. Sudden feelings of insecurity can overtake even the most emotionally healthy person at times. This is a very complex and multifaceted subject. However, the lack of the secure anchor of self-esteem can be a significant contributing factor to feelings of insecurity.

Developing self-esteem is not the same as becoming self-absorbed or selfish.

Has your self-esteem been affected by years of disingenuous people pleasing? Licensed Christian counselor Bernis Riley said this in her questionnaire:

People with low self-esteem have their major difficulties in relationships with others. A person with low self-esteem does not properly value herself or himself. Therefore, they look for external things or people to give them value. They then become enslaved to how others perceive them.

People with low self-esteem have weakened internal controls and become dependent on strong external controls. They are easily controlled by the way others think and feel about them and act toward them. People with low self-esteem depend on others' approval and recognition and are therefore fearful of conflict with and rejection by others.

In her book *Downside Up*, author Tracey Mitchell concurs that it can be difficult to say no because of our fear of being rejected.

> A person who fears rejection often develops a people-pleasing personality. Eager to gain or keep the approval of others, they fall into an approval-based performance trap. For some, the need for acceptance is so strong they adapt their personality to fit the role or image others find desirable. Becoming emotional actors or actresses, they take on roles of various personalities, professions, occupations, or even false identities, if it means gaining the approval of another. They willingly do whatever it takes to make others happy. This identity crisis often continues until they grow weary of playing the part and subsequently begin to blame others for forcing them to become something they are not.[1]

The Fallout of Fear

The third debilitating feeling we can experience when we have boudary-related challenges is fear. When we live in the fullness of God's grace and love, we can recognize our personal needs and assume responsibility to seek ways to meet them appropriately. We all need to feel security, significance, and love. The need for our heart to be healthy is critical because everything we do flows from it. Why is it so many women seem to have lost the ability to walk boldly in God's will? To stand confidently in our identity and purpose? Why do we fear that we will dishonor and disappoint God by not saying yes every time we are asked to help? What is it we really fear? We fear...

- being rejected
- feeling worthless
- being abused
- being unloved
- appearing selfish
- appearing self-centered
- being alone
- letting someone down
- the unknown
- change
- being labeled negatively
- not being a good Christian

Clearly, this list could go on and on. We fear a great many things, including the consequences of seeking to have our own needs met, which can be scary for some of us. However, while facing our fears may usher in a season of uncomfortable unknowns, it can also be the start of something miraculous.

Saying Yes with Love

Setting healthy boundaries and finding peace in life isn't just about how firm we are in saying no. It's really about our willingness to make intentional choices based on saying yes truthfully.

Saying yes is a good thing, especially when we authentically desire to bless someone. The Bible says, "Dear children, let us not love with words or speech but with actions and in truth" (1 John 3:18). "Dear friends, since God so loved us, we also ought to love one another" (1 John 4:11). Columnist Martha Beck makes this note:

> Some psychologists classify every emotion as either love (attraction) or fear (aversion). It's not unusual for humans to base almost every decision on fear: fear of rejection, fear of poverty, fear of looking dumb, and so on. But after coaching thousands of people, I've seen that fear-based

decisions lead to hollow victories at best, endless regret at worst. Only love-based decisions create lasting happiness.[2]

It's good when we can make love-based decisions, when we can say yes based on authentic love and ability and not from a place of guilt, insecurity, or fear.

Additionally, God often calls us to sacrifice. Saying yes might not feel good, but we may know in our spirit that it *is* good and that it's how we are being called to respond.

Therefore, I'm going to propose that instead of trying to find the courage to say no, let's switch our thinking. Let's look instead at saying yes authentically with love for the Lord, for others, and for ourselves.

> We need to establish acceptable boundaries for the way people treat us. We must learn to say no without guilt and yes from an authentic place of love and ability.

We can walk confidently in power and with purpose when we say yes or no in obedience to God with authentic hearts—protected hearts.

If we truly want to find peace and live in a way that pleases God, we need to take a stand for our lives. We cannot change other people, but we can change the way we respond to them and to the way they treat us. We need to establish acceptable boundaries for the way people treat us. We must learn to say no without guilt and yes from an authentic place of love and ability.

When we're intentionally making choices to change the way we think, feel, and respond, we also need to pray for wisdom and discernment. Then we must listen for God's responses and trust Him.

If you have a problem saying no or tend to overcommit yourself by saying yes, declare from this day forward that when you're in doubt about your yes or no, you will take prayerful control of your life and first ask God how you should respond. Declare that you will ask the

Holy Spirit to reveal His truth to you and that you will listen to that truth as you apply the "T" Step in SANITY and *Trust the Voice of the Spirit.* This is a hand-in-glove partnership of our prayers and His responses.

For example, you might respond differently the next time you're asked to help. You could say, "Thank you for asking. I really want to help you with [fill in the blank], but I've made a promise to myself that before I say yes to anything, I will pray about it first. Can I get back to you on this?"

Contrary to the lie the enemy wants us to believe, taking control of our lives in this manner isn't a selfish pursuit. In fact, when we have trouble saying no or saying yes for the wrong reasons, it's wise to ask God to intercede on our behalf and give us a proper perspective of the situations and circumstances in our lives. Authors Henry T. Blackaby and Claude V. King offer this counsel:

> Our experiences alone cannot be our guide. Every experience must be controlled and understood by the Scriptures. The God revealed in Scripture does not change. Throughout your life, you will have times when you want to respond based on your experiences or your wisdom. Seeking to know God's will based on circumstances alone can be misleading. This should be your guideline: Always go back to the Bible for truth (or for the Holy Spirit to reveal truth). [3]

When you begin to develop new responses to people's requests for help, be prepared for varying degrees of acceptance (or resistance). Many of us have already set the precedent for being Dependable Debbie or Reliable Rita, and just because we're changing our responses doesn't mean everyone is going to be happy about it.

People who are able to set healthy boundaries for themselves may initially be surprised that you're taking control of your life in such an intentional manner. These folks will respect and admire your thoughtful response. However, those who have boundary issues of their own and those who have come to depend on your yes in the past may become defensive or even angry. Be aware that these negative responses from others will most likely trigger a host of feelings and emotions in you that can blindside your sincere motivation if you're not careful.

Deciding When to Say Yes or No

- We say no when someone or something hurts us.
- We say no when something goes against the will of God.
- We say no when the Voice of the Spirit reveals truth and convicts us to do so.
- We say *yes* when the Voice of the Spirit reveals truth and convicts us to do so.

Saying No to Insanity

Life can change when we begin to use the SANITY Steps as tools to help us make different choices.

We've established that a critical component in setting healthy boundaries is to guard, protect, and prepare our hearts as we face our own negative behavior and destructive patterns. This may include learning how to say no in a firm and loving manner, changing our perspective on control, and exploring our emotions, motivations, and expectations. Hope grows as we learn to depend on God to help us make choices that will change our lives and not perpetuate the status quo—the insanity of living on the gerbil wheel.

If we're unable to say no with calm authority or yes with heartfelt authenticity, the price we pay is low self-esteem, depression, a sense of being overwhelmed, burnout, high stress levels, and possibly other physical, emotional, and spiritual ailments. Some of our relationships may be in serious jeopardy. Others may already have been destroyed.

Additionally, when we find it hard to say no, we don't allow others to step up to the plate and find their own power and purpose. In that case, our helping is actually hurting.

When all is said and done, our words need to be authentic and aligned with what God is telling us in our spirit. We say goodbye to insanity when we learn how to say what we mean and mean what we say. That level of conviction comes only when we walk in true spiritual authority.

A SANITY Prayer

Lord, You know how hard it is for me to say no. I often agree to more things than I should. I am often frazzled, frustrated, and fearful that I will be unable to accomplish everything, and sometimes my results are lacking because of this. I'm tired of feeling guilty and angry at myself for not being able to say no. I'm tired of feeling angry at the people who make the requests in the first place. After all, they aren't responsible to set healthy boundaries for me. Help me to understand what is my responsibility and what isn't. Help me learn to say yes and no for the right reasons and in ways that please You. Amen.

9

Expectations Can Be Exhausting

So many factors make up a person's humanity. We can expect something like our natural-born temperament to remain with us for life, but it's good to remember that we are molded by circumstances, environment, coping styles, experiences, influences, and of course our choices. Therefore, our expectations can be tied to a great many issues, including our emotions, motivation, and identity. Additionally, a great deal of expectation comes from the way we were raised.

We'll talk more later about personality temperaments and how they may affect our expectations, but for now let's focus on the importance of having reasonable expectations as we establish healthy boundaries and find SANITY. Our sinful nature and the lying schemes of the enemy work against us in this area, so it's important to consider our expectations from a spiritual perspective. Author Virelle Kidder responded to my questionnaire by writing this:

> My mother's expectations and emotional neediness controlled our home and much of my life until I was in my fifties. Sad, but true. A Christian counselor straightened me out in one hour by explaining the difference between what God expects of me and what my mother expected of me. Two different things entirely. The relief was immediate.

Tears flowed as the enormous weight I'd been chained to forever was loosened.

When we've been repeatedly exposed to unreasonable expectations, or when we develop a highly responsible, performance-oriented mind-set, we can easily develop unreasonable expectations for ourselves and for others. However, God doesn't demand perfection from us. God isn't expecting us to measure up. He has never expected us to live the Christian life on our own or meet His holy standards. If He thought we could, He wouldn't have sent Jesus to earth to die for us. But He did.

God wants us to be free from bondage, to enjoy the freedom and love of being in relationship with Him. He wants us to live according to what He says is right, to experience His bountiful love and have joy as Christians.

Yet we struggle to find joy in life when our expectations for others and ourselves are out of balance. When it comes to expectations, I've found there are three primary types:

- reasonable (justifiable)
- unreasonable or unrealistic (impossible)
- different (individual)

Of course, some expectations are entirely reasonable, such as expecting a spouse to be faithful, expecting a child who lives under your roof to be respectful and obedient, or expecting to receive a paycheck at the end of the pay period. It's also thoroughly reasonable to expect people not to treat us with physical, emotional, or verbal abuse.

However, our expectations can become problematic when they become unreasonable or unrealistic. We wouldn't expect toddlers to understand the consequences of their actions. We wouldn't expect habitual drug abusers to respect our personal property. And we shouldn't expect ourselves or others to be perfect. If we're not careful, unrealistic expectations can set us up for failure and leave lasting scars on our hearts.

This critical area of reasonable versus unreasonable expectations gives people like Dr. Phil a never-ending list of clients. If you listen closely to the guests who talk about their relational problems on his program, you'll see that they share a common cause—unmet expectations.

We all have different realities. Each of us has a unique set of expectations, and that can make setting boundaries difficult for some of us, as Dr. Jill Hubbard explains.

> We women have a keen sense of needing to live up to expectations—those from our families, our culture, our Christian community, and those we place on ourselves. We tend to have unrealistic expectations about what we *should* be able to accomplish and about what life was going to be like. But life usually doesn't follow our expectations. Often, our experience of reality doesn't match with what we've been led to believe our reality should be. So we hide our reality. [1]

Hiding our reality, especially for a long time, can result in a multitude of boundary-related challenges.

Differing Expectations

People have various expectations of the way respect, loyalty, forgiveness, dependability, work ethic, promptness, commitment, and such things should be expressed in a relationship. For example, I always try to arrive a few minutes early for appointments, but I have a friend who thinks he's being prompt if he's no more than 15 minutes late for an appointment. Clearly we have very different expectations of what it means to be prompt.

Someone may expect family members to be loyal to one another, but someone else in the family may not share that expectation. The first person is set up to be disappointed. We move toward SANITY when we realize that people don't always think alike and share the same expectations.

The joy of diversity is a blessing, but our differences can bring some of the most complicated challenges to the surface. However, this is life, and having different opinions, choices, and expectation is natural. That's why it's important to stop, step back, and pray about your response when something begins to feel uncomfortable. If you feel prompted by the Holy Spirit that your expectations are reasonable, you can speak the truth in love and set a healthy boundary.

Spiritual Expectations

Our primary relationship is with God, who lives in us and produces good works in and through us. We want to live in ways that please Him, but we can't expect to do this on our own. We must ask God to build this ability into our lives through His Spirit, to empower us to obey Him. We obey His commands by relying on Him.

We must ask Him to change our thinking or work in our lives in whatever way He needs to so that our lives can line up with His desires for us.

God has desires, or expectations, for all of us. He has a plan for our lives—to use our lives to benefit others for His glory. However, He's not expecting us to perform for Him. The Bible says, "It is by grace you have been saved, through faith—and this is not from yourselves, it is the gift of God—not by works, so that no one can boast. For we are God's handiwork, created in Christ Jesus to do good works, which God prepared in advance for us to do" (Ephesians 2:8-10).

Negative Expectations

We can exhaust ourselves by expecting others to respond to situations the same way we would. Have you ever said, "I can't believe she did that! I would never even *think* of doing something like that!"

Conversely, always expecting the worst from others can also put a damper on relationships. If past interactions, choices, or mistakes have left us damaged or bruised, our self-preservation mode is likely to kick in. We're more likely to remember betrayals than positive interactions, so we often underestimate people's sincerity and generosity and overestimate their selfishness. In other words, our expectations are often based on our own cynicism, negativity, and judgment.

So we must find a delicate balance. On one hand, we want to live in a place of trust, love, and reasonable expectations and not become cynical or jaded. On the other hand, we live in a world where people don't live up to our expectations and sometimes hurt us.

Trusting no one or having low expectations for ourselves can be exhausting. We may feel we aren't worthy, able, or capable. Low self-expectation can greatly affect us, especially if we are unclear about our identity in Christ.

The Lord doesn't judge us by arbitrary standards that change with current trends. His Word remains steadfast and true in all ways for always, and He loves us with an unfailing love.

The Expectation of Love

Marie and Scott have been married for six years and have three children, ages five, three and one. Marie is a hands-on stay-at-home mom. She is 28 years old and pregnant with their fourth child, which means she has been pregnant for most of their marriage. Scott is 30 and is the co-owner of a small but successful construction company. They have a beautiful home, and both of them work hard in handling their responsibilities.

Marie is soft-spoken and loving with a people-pleasing personality. Scott is a kind and thoughtful man with a more serious nature. He's also a generous husband and often buys Marie designer handbags, clothing, and nice jewelry. In fact, he just bought her a new Lincoln Navigator.

Their home is neat and clean. Dishes never stack up on the counter or in the sink because Marie promptly puts them in the dishwasher or washes them immediately. She is forever washing, folding, and putting away clothes and linens. Marie has efficient systems for organization, the kids have bins for their toys, and everything has a place. She's careful to keep things put away and encourages her youngsters to do the same. She dresses nicely and takes good care of herself even though she feels exhausted much of the time.

Scott's day begins early. He is typically out of the house before Marie and the children are up. He has multiple building sites to visit throughout the day, supplies to purchase and sometimes deliver, clients to meet, and work to handle back at the office. His days are long, but he is usually home for dinner by seven. Marie eats earlier with the children but always prepares a plate for Scott.

The kids are usually bathed and in bed by the time he returns home, but he looks forward to tucking them in and saying good night if they're still awake. Marie will often sit with Scott as he eats dinner. They talk about their days while she's folding clothes or mending, ironing, or baking something for the next day.

Scott and Marie are both overachievers with high expectations for themselves and for others. However, Scott has recently developed extremely critical expectations for what Marie should be doing all day and how the house should look when he comes home. He's begun a new habit of walking through the entire house before going to bed as though he were inspecting one of his building sites. But instead of looking for construction issues, he's looking for things that are out of place or tasks that he expects Marie to accomplish the next day, tasks he writes down on an actual to-do list for her.

Marie resents Scott's list and says, "I have three kids at home, two of them still in diapers, and I'm pregnant—it's all I can do to have the clothes washed, the house clean, food in the refrigerator, and dinner on the table when Scott comes home. Things are pretty organized around here, and I go nonstop from sunup until long after sundown. I know Scott works hard as well, but he has no idea what my days are like. He's become quite critical. If he sees even one toy on the floor when he gets home, he starts inferring that I'm being lazy. And if, heaven forbid, I'm sitting on the sofa with my feet up watching TV when he walks in, you'd think I was committing a capital crime. I'm eight months pregnant, for crying out loud! And he keeps bringing up the things he buys—as if he's paying me for housekeeping services I'm not rendering. I never know what's going to set him off these days, and I'm tired of walking on eggshells and arguing with him. I'm beginning to feel that I can't do anything right. No matter how hard I try, it's never going to be good enough for him."

Scott's increasingly unreasonable expectations for Marie are beginning to border on abusiveness, and they are causing extreme friction in their relationship.

Marie's and Scott's opposing expectations are leading them into dangerous territory, and if they want to have a healthy marriage, healthy kids, and a healthy faith, they need to reach a healthy compromise by developing reasonable expectations.

Clearly, though, something deeper is going on in the relationship that has Scott suddenly being so critical of Marie. This isn't about a few toys being out of place or Marie watching TV after a long day. She's eight months pregnant, raising three children, and running a well-organized household. Something else is going on.

We all have emotional triggers that can cause us to respond in unhealthy ways or prohibit us from acting in healthy ways. Discovering what is motivating Scott's behavior is important, and communicating effectively is critical for the health and safety of their marriage.

God has a unique plan for Scott and Marie individually, as husband and wife, as parents to young children, and as stewards of the blessings He has given them.

Marie has to be prayerful about setting a healthy boundary with firmness and love. She can't ignore Scott's unreasonable expectations and increasing verbal abuse. She knows that keeping silent and pretending the growing problem doesn't exist isn't the best approach, and she is fervently praying for God's wisdom.

Unspoken Expectations

Leeann belongs to a small but growing community church. She operates an in-home day care center for 10 to 15 children, including babies and toddlers. This is an enormous responsibility. Leann is also an excellent baker. Her pastries and confections have held center court at countless holiday events and celebrations at her church.

However, if you were a fly on the wall in her kitchen, you would hear Leeann complain loudly when she's asked to prepare one of her signature dishes.

"Just because I work from home doesn't mean I have time to bake all day. It takes a lot to prepare and cook these dishes. People have no idea, but they always expect me to say yes. Why can't somebody else do it?"

Indeed. Why can't someone else do it? Could one reason be that Leanne never says no when she's asked?

Many women are wonderfully gifted cooks, bakers, decorators, hostesses, and teachers. But when these women are bound by other people's expectations, they often become ineffective in ministry, and their families and churches suffer dissension. The enemy has convinced many of us that our organizations can't function if we don't come to the rescue and help with our gifts and talents.

It's good to help—but are we really helping? Could our consistent involvement in some areas be denying others the opportunity to develop and share their gifts and talents?

The issue isn't whether we're capable of doing a project. Of course we're able. Rather, it's whether God is actually calling us to do it—if it's truly His will for our lives. Or are we driven by our own need for acceptance and appreciation? Is our decision love-based or fear-based?

Leeann thought it was unreasonable for her church to consistently expect her to bake every time a hot dish was needed. But how would they know that? The church felt blessed that she was always ready, willing, and able to help. They had no idea that much of the time she was doing so begrudgingly—and building up quite a bit of resentment along the way.

"They're taking advantage of me," she said as she placed another casserole dish into the oven for a sick church member, the third this week, and returned to preparing lunch for the 15 children in her care.

By stewing in silence, Leeann wasn't being truthful to herself or to her church. Her unspoken expectation was that the church should ask her to bake once or twice a month, not every time there was a need. On the other hand, her church assumed that she would feel insulted and be upset if she wasn't the first person they called when a need arose. They never realized that her yes wasn't authentic.

Neither set of expectations was unreasonable. They were just different, and no one took control in a God-honoring way and spoke up.

Vocalizing Expectations

Stacy and Roger were high school sweethearts who married after college. They worked several part-time jobs, budgeted their income, and saved wisely in order to travel and experience the world before having children and raising a family. They were thrilled when Roger was offered a part-time position as the youth pastor at their small church. However, they were surprised to discover that many in their congregation didn't approve of their intentional decision to wait before starting a family. In fact, because of several outspoken church members, Stacy began to feel guilty about their choices, and she struggled for a time with feelings of selfishness and wrongdoing.

"It was as if I had a shelf life that was about to expire," she said. "We've only been married for three years, but apparently this community expected, 'First comes love, then comes marriage, then come Roger and Stacy with a baby carriage.' And the sooner the better. Besides, I felt that discussing my reproductive capabilities was totally unacceptable, yet these women felt comfortable crossing this boundary and asking some very personal things. My initial reaction was to defend myself, but the Spirit brought to mind the SANITY analogy, and I stopped myself from responding in a way that could be misunderstood or misconstrued. I talked with Roger about my feelings, and we prayed about the situation."

They also sought input from close advisers, including their parents, and they decided to verbally address their entire congregation after a Sunday service. Here is what they said.

"We love all of you so very much. We feel blessed that God has called us to be part of this church family. It will be an honor and a privilege to raise our children in this family. However, we have made a prayerful choice to wait to be parents, and we respectfully ask that you consider the possibility that our call and yours may be different. You'll be some of the first to know should we find ourselves expecting, but until that time, we would be so thankful if you would allow us to keep this issue private between the two of us."

A few members were upset that they were being asked to stop over-stepping boundaries and asking questions. It's impossible to please everyone all of the time. But the majority of the congregation was supportive and understanding. A few even apologized privately to Stacy. Sometimes our choice to set healthy boundaries allows others to be their best selves.

The Root of Expectation

When we face situations that are unsettling, uncomfortable, confusing, or chaotic, the way we respond is critical to the outcome.

Scott and Marie are a good example for doing this right. They love each other very much, but something was wrong, a deeper emotional issue from the past or the present, and they needed to address it with God's help.

Fortunately, Marie heard about the SANITY Steps and began to apply them to her thoughts, actions, and responses. Instead of defending herself, arguing, and getting hurt by Scott's nightly home inspections and his to-do lists, one night she greeted him at the door and asked if she could say a prayer that the Lord had placed on her heart. She had prayed about this prayer throughout the day and didn't cast blame on anyone. She held Scott's hands in hers and quietly said, "Dear Lord, thank You for bringing my husband safely home. Thank You for the blessing of healthy children, a healthy marriage, and a lovely home.

Please help us to walk in Your will and reveal to us the ways we can be good and loving parents and spouses. Amen."

She refused to say a negative word when he criticized anything about her or the house, and she repeated this same simple prayer every night for several days. Eventually, she began to notice that Scott's critical spirit was starting to soften. One night as he ate dinner and they talked about the new baby, the Lord convicted Scott of his recent actions and broke his heart. That was when Marie learned what was really at the core of these unreasonable expectations.

Scott's parents were deceased when he met Marie, and he had never talked much about them. Finally, he revealed that his childhood was chaotic and caustic. When his alcoholic father died of liver failure, his mother became an extreme hoarder. The problem became so bad that the state removed him from the house when he was 12, and he was in foster care until he "aged out" of the system. His mother died a few years later.

"I didn't think much about it until I was having lunch with the guys one day last month," Scott told Marie. "One of those hoarder shows was on the TV, and they started saying things like the show was fixed and no one could live like that. But we did. Then at one of the job sites later the same day, I saw this woman who looked just like my mother, and all of a sudden I couldn't stop thinking about anything else, day in and day out. Marie, I don't know what got into me about our house… you do a really good job, honey. I'm so sorry…"

This story had a happy ending, but it could have taken an entirely different turn. Unhealthy emotions can lead to unreasonable expectations, and when no one is ready, willing, or able to take control in a God-honoring way to stop the insanity, relationships can suffer.

Getting to the root of your expectations, communicating openly with your loved ones, and praying for them—these are critical in your journey to find peace.

How have expectations affected your life? Grab your notebook and divide a page into three columns with the headings Reasonable,

Unreasonable, and Different. Then start writing. What unreasonable or unrealistic expectations do you need to let go of? What reasonable ones do you need to cultivate? Consider your family and friends—how do their expectations differ from yours? How can you create a healthy compromise? Pray about each of these areas.

In many instances, the words "boundary" and "expectation" are interchangeable.

You will find peace when you have reasonable expectations and make heartfelt and authentic decisions based on your faith—on walking in God's will for your life. Sometimes, those decisions come easily. Other times, they are difficult and painful.

Our expectations are shaped by our personality, emotions, and motivations, and the better we understand those aspects of who we are, the easier it is to have healthy and reasonable expectations for ourselves and others.

10

Personality, Emotions, and Motivations

Why do people cope with similar life experiences in different ways? For example, two siblings with the same abusive parents may respond very differently. One becomes a passive, frightened victim and remains that way throughout life. The other child becomes openly rebellious and defiant and may even leave home early to survive as a teenager on the streets.

In this chapter I'll point to three possible reasons why we behave the way we do and how they affect our boundaries. These three factors are personality traits, emotions, and motivations.

Inborn Personality Traits

Much of what becomes "us" as we grow is a result of inborn traits that vary from person to person, even within the same family. One sibling may be quiet, withdrawn, and sensitive, while another sibling may be the life of the party. Of course, the way we're raised will contribute to the way those natural personality traits are shaped. For instance, one child may unconsciously choose one parent and not the other as a role model. We often see this when an abuser marries a victim. Their children could model either parent or both.

Interaction with peers also shapes the basic personality. The shy introverted child may blossom if he or she is respected by peers. Or the child may be teased mercilessly for being shy, which could have a negative effect on a developing personality.

Whatever the scenario, by the time we reach adulthood we've become a conglomeration of elements. Our personality has been molded by circumstances, environment, coping styles, emotions, motivations, experiences, influences, and our choices. However, whatever the years may bring, our natural temperament remains.

In my early walk of faith, I was given a copy of *The Spirit-Controlled Woman* by Beverly LaHaye. This was the first time I'd considered the temperaments from a Christian perspective, and I learned how the Holy Spirit can maximize and minimize these attributes to fulfill God's purpose. As a professional fund-raiser in Southern California at the time, I was quite familiar with the various personality assessment tools, especially the Myers-Briggs Type Indicator (I'm an ENTJ). In our staff meetings, we commonly discussed our advisory board members by their personality types. We understood the dynamics of personalities and matched our volunteers accordingly (particularly the philanthropic powerhouses) to ensure good synergy among committees.

My second introduction to the way our inborn temperaments affect us was through Florence Littauer, founder of Christian Leaders, Authors, and Speakers (CLASS). In her excellent book *Personality Plus*, Florence puts her own imprint on the temperaments.

> We were all born with our own temperament traits, our raw material, our own kind of rock. Some of us are granite, some marble, some alabaster, some sandstone. Our type of rock doesn't change, but our shapes can be altered. So it is with our personalities. We start with our own set of inborn traits. Some of our qualities are beautiful with strains of gold. Some are blemished with fault lines of gray. Our circumstances, IQ, nationality, economics, environment, and parental influences can mold our personalities, but the rock underneath remains the same.[1]

Florence teaches that understanding the differences in our basic temperaments takes the pressure off our relationships. She says life will change when we can look at each other's differences in a positive way and not try to make everyone be like us. She highlights two critical things about the temperaments that can change our lives.

1. We must examine our own strengths and weaknesses and learn how to accentuate our positives and eliminate our negatives.

2. We must understand other people and realize that being different from us does not make them wrong.

The Greek physician Hippocrates identified four basic temperaments 400 years before Christ was born. Many contemporary authors follow these four basic temperaments.

Hippocrates	Beverly LaHaye and Florence Littauer
sanguine	popular sanguine
choleric	powerful choleric
phlegmatic	peaceful phlegmatic
melancholic	perfect melancholy

A Different Personality, a Different Perspective

If you know anything about the four temperaments, you don't need to be around me long to see I'm a powerful choleric—a dominant personality. We're known to be leaders, organizers, and communicators. We're goal oriented but not necessarily relationship oriented. This doesn't mean I don't need or want relationships. It just means the way I perceive and develop them is different from the way other personality types do. Keep in mind that every temperament has both strengths and weaknesses.

Do you know your personality type? If not, I encourage you to do some reading on this topic. Florence Littauer's book is a great place to start. It may help you in setting your boundaries. Insight into the strengths and weaknesses of your personality can be valuable, especially when considering what motivates us to do the things we do in life. Could some aspects of our inborn temperament predispose us to respond to others in certain ways? If so, what can we do to accentuate the positive and tone down the negative?

This topic has fascinated me over the years. The knowledge I've gained has been helpful in both my personal and professional life. The same can be true for you.

I'm aware that I have a powerful personality type, so I know I can often appear overly confident and somewhat forceful, especially to people with more subdued personality traits. Additionally, because of the abuse in my past and my other life experience and influences, I can sometimes get defensive, side-tracked, and confused in my relationship responses. I pray often for God to soften my sharp edges and to give me wisdom and discernment concerning my natural inclination to be in control—which is very much a trait of my particular personality type. I also ask Him to show me what He really does want me to control.

> We can't please others all the time. We simply cannot make everyone happy. God didn't call us to be everything to everybody here on earth.

Life experiences add color and texture to who we become, but every personality type has distinct traits that may rub others the wrong way regardless of what we say or do.

We can't please others all the time. We simply cannot make everyone happy. God didn't call us to be everything to everybody here on earth. That's an unrealistic and exhausting expectation. However, we are more than enough to Jesus, and He loves us regardless of how many weaknesses we have, how many mistakes we make, and how much trouble we have setting boundaries.

Could your natural-born temperament include inherent weaknesses that hinder your ability to set healthy boundaries and take control? Could this be one reason for the lack of peace in your life? Are you using the strengths of your temperament to bring glory and honor to God? To produce fruit from your labor? Or are you allowing the weaknesses to prohibit you from making a difference? To keep you from fulfilling the plan and purpose God has for you?

The Control Aspect of Every Personality

Being in control is not the same as being controlling. Understanding this will help us be willing and able to set healthy boundaries.

Self-preservation is a natural inclination of every living creature. Very few people will relinquish control when faced with death or destruction. Most of us will fight with every fiber of our being to survive. However, the way we demonstrate that fight depends on our personality type.

We all take control differently. Our personality type may lead us toward identifiable strengths or weaknesses, but God can always work as the ultimate controlling influence to help us find balance. He knows exactly who we are and what our strengths and weaknesses are. He has been watching over us, caring for us, and pruning us since before we were born. The Bible says, "He will take great delight in you; in his love he will no longer rebuke you, but will rejoice over you with singing" (Zephaniah 3:17).

Isn't that a beautiful picture—to think of God singing over us?

A Different Perspective

It's good to remember that the very things someone finds exhilarating about your communication style or personality temperament might be the same things that someone else struggles with. That doesn't necessarily mean you are wrong.

For example, one of my dearest friends told me one of the things she admires and respects the most about me is that I speak up when something is bothering me.

"I always know where I stand with you," she said. "I can trust that about you, and I like that kind of dependability in our friendship. I admire you for who you are."

This was encouraging because I once overheard a woman I barely knew say quite the opposite. Perhaps I reminded this woman of someone or something that flipped an emotional trigger, or maybe our inherent personality types were radically opposite. Whatever the case, that didn't stop me from wanting to defend myself. But once again, we cannot be everything to everybody. We need to own who we are, whose we are, and where we come from. As we embrace the most important relationship in life and grow in God's grace, we must pray that God will mold and shape us into the people He wants us to be.

This isn't the place to discuss all the various characteristics of the four personality temperaments, so I encourage you to pick up one of the resources I've mentioned in this chapter, such as Beverly LaHaye's *The New Spirit-Controlled Woman* or Florence Littauer's *Personality Plus*.

Let's pray for wisdom and discernment to approach the subject of emotions, motivations, and temperaments in a way that honors God, protects our hearts, and brings us peace.

Emotions

We each have a unique set of emotions. Like our temperaments, our emotions can cause us to react to situations in unique ways.

Our emotions are part of what makes us human beings. An emotionless life would be less than life. Our emotions are necessary for our survival. And when we have weak or nonexistent boundaries, we need to understand that our negative emotional responses aren't the problem. They're merely the indication of a problem.

If you have a brother or sister who drives you crazy, a coworker who has you considering quitting, an ex-spouse making child visitation a nightmare, or a friend from church whose gossip is keeping you from attending Sunday service, you need to do more than simply construct a new personal boundary to protect yourself. Yes, that's a critical start, but you also need to gain a better understanding of your emotions—what you're thinking and feeling about your challenging relationship with this person. What emotional trigger is this person or this situation pulling in you? (A careful consideration of his or her personality and emotional makeup may also be revealing.)

I love what Donna Carter writes about emotions in her book *10 Smart Things Women Can Do to Build a Better Life*.

> Our emotional world is one of the most difficult parts of our lives to manage. We think we're in complete control, but then something or someone pushes our buttons and our emotions go from 0 to 60 faster than a Porsche. Later, in the aftermath, we wonder, "What was that all about?" [2]

Indeed…what is it all about? For many of us, this is the million-dollar question.

Emotions Are Signals

Sad to say, negative emotions outnumber positive ones. People can feel fear, anger, shame, and hate, and yet beyond happiness and joy, there are few other positive feelings. This is because most emotions are designed to keep us alive. They signal danger and prompt us to act, to run away, or to fight back. Without emotions we wouldn't survive very long.

Emotions are signals that tell us something about what's happening inside us. This can be very useful because we often don't realize what's going on in that deep and dark subconscious inside of us. An awareness of our own emotions and emotional triggers helps us understand what makes us tick.

So, what *does* make us tick?

Unfortunately, some boundary violations can scar us for life. We can be injured physically, emotionally, sexually, and even spiritually. These injuries often shape who we become. We develop coping and defensive strategies very early in life, and sometimes we don't see how our current habits and behaviors are based on those early dynamics.

If you were terrorized by a large vicious dog when you were a kid, your present fear of large dogs makes perfect sense. However, some reactions are more difficult to understand. Perhaps you witnessed your father terrorizing your fearful mother. Could that be one reason you now take the role of a people-pleaser—to avoid any type of conflict whatsoever? Or maybe you were the oldest daughter in a family of six. When your mother died and your father checked out emotionally, you had to raise your siblings. Could that be why you now feel an exaggerated sense of responsibility for everyone and everything in your life?

Unfortunately, many of us are casualties of a less than perfect childhood. However, that doesn't mean we are destined to live in the shadow of our past. We can work through the deep internal struggles and emotional messes that we haven't wanted to address. Despite our past, we still can become confident, optimistic, and hopeful women.

When I reflect on my life journey, I'm struck by God's ability to make broken things new—to empower ordinary people to do extraordinary things through His love. It's not about me or you. It's about what He does through us. Our part is to identify the enemy's strongholds—the lies that keep us in bondage. When I eliminated the lies of the enemy with God's truth, which speaks directly to my heart and soul, my life changed. So can yours!

Learning to set healthy boundaries as an adult can feel uncomfortable and even scary because it may go against the grain of the survival skills we learned in childhood. This is especially true if our caretakers were physically, sexually, or emotionally abusive. For example, we may have learned to repress our anger or other painful emotions to avoid being attacked again. Thus, our attempts to set healthy boundaries as adults may initially cause anxiety, but we must learn to work through these conditioned fears. Otherwise we will never have healthy relationships. We will never have peace.

In all instances, we must find the underlying cause of our issues in order to begin releasing the pain. Getting down to that root requires an intentional exploration of our emotions and motivations.

Understanding Emotions

What is the purpose of emotions? They certainly have a significant effect on us, but what is it all for? When we feel emotionally, we also feel physically. Our emotions can make us feel uncomfortable or comfortable, sending us signals to do something urgently or to stay in our comfortable state. Emotions motivate us, and motivations are felt in the body. Motivations are our goals, drives, desires, and needs. They are often outside our conscious awareness, so they're difficult to identify and even more difficult to manage and target for change.

Remember Margaret? Within a 24-hour period, her husband left her for another woman, and her teenage son stole $500 from her checking account and was arrested on a DUI charge. Margaret was stunned. Her emotions cut through her heart like a tornado cuts through a town. She felt frightened and betrayed. She was petrified to be alone. This was motivating her to consider borrowing money to bail her son out of jail. She wanted him to come home and protect her—to make her feel safe.

But this wasn't his responsibility. He was addicted to drugs and needed emotional help, and he was facing serious criminal charges. He was in no condition to meet her needs. She knew that, but her emotions threatened to override her intellect. Unfortunately, women often ignore this state of mind, especially when our internal and social signals have gone haywire after years of neglect.

Internal Signals

Remember, emotions are powerful signals. When we're trying to understand something or make a decision, our emotions can help us determine whether our conclusions are valid. For example, when we think about something that contradicts our values, our emotions will tell us it is bad. When we think about something that could hurt us, our emotions will tell us it isn't a good idea. Simply imagining what might happen triggers emotions that can help us make better decisions.

At least that's the way it is supposed to work.

This speaks directly to the universal law of cause and effect—for every action there is a reaction or response. The energy of our intentions flows outward, affecting many other people. Therefore we need to speak, think, and behave with great thoughtfulness and compassion. We need to say what we mean and mean what we say with firmness and love.

Sadly, like Margaret, we have sent negative energy outward by ignoring our internal signals or overreacting to them, thus responding poorly. But when we *Stop Our Own Negative Behavior* and *Trust the Voice of the Spirit*, we can often recognize that these responses are wrong.

Margaret repeatedly accepted unacceptable behavior from her son and husband by never setting healthy boundaries. Her responses to their negative behavior were just as negative. She would get overly emotional, make excuses for them, blame herself, or adopt a victim mentality. Margaret was so accustomed to ignoring (invalidating) her emotions, she had disabled her ability to make value-based, God-honoring decisions.

Social Signals

When emotions are used as social signals, they help people decide how to behave toward each other. This is generally very useful. If someone is looking angry, approaching him for a favor might not be a good idea. If he is looking afraid, perhaps he needs help. We generally wear our hearts on our sleeves. Our inner emotions are often displayed on our outer bodies. Our faces, in particular, have around 90 muscles, 30 of which have the sole purpose of signaling emotions to other people, such as anger, sadness, fear, and joy.

Margaret had spent years looking sad, fearful, and weak—social signals that her dysfunctional family members interpreted as invitations to disrespect and disregard her.

Margaret began to find peace when she admitted that although her previous choices were not always helpful, it wasn't too late to change the trajectory of her life.

The Emotions That Drive Us

Viewing our emotions as signals from God can be a powerful tool in helping us to understand what is going on inside of us.

In essence, emotions keep us alive. That doesn't mean we're alive because we have emotions. We're alive because God created us. God is the author of life and the Creator of our emotions. We are born with God-given emotional needs for love, significance, and security, and God can help us understand and calm our emotions. The Bible says, "Before I formed you in the womb I knew you, before you were born I set you apart; I appointed you as a prophet to the nations" (Jeremiah 1:5).

Review this list of four emotions and their opposites below. What emotions typically motivate your responses or reaction to others? Use your notebook and write down your thoughts. Include specific incidents you can recall where these emotions played a part.

Emotion	Opposite
joy	sadness
trust	disgust
fear	anger
surprise	anticipation

Take some time on this writing exercise and stop to ask God to shine light on the emotions that seem to control you most often. Write down some recent incidents in your life and identify your emotional responses.

Motivational Murkiness

God gave us our emotions, but where did our motives come from? These are a third possible cause for the way we react to life's events.

Drs. Cloud and Townsend believe we often fail to set boundaries because we have *false motives* for doing what we do. We often give (or "help") for all the wrong reasons. After closer scrutiny, we may find that our motive for giving wasn't love, but the fear of losing love.

We might say, "I'm helping my daughter with [fill in the blank] because I love her." But we might really mean, "I'm helping my daughter [fill in the blank] because if I don't, she won't love me. She'll probably move out of the house, and I'm afraid to be alone." Or we might say, "I'm going to bail my brother out of jail again because I love him." But we might really mean, "I'm going to bail my brother out of jail again because if I don't, my mom and dad will never forgive me."

Many parents are discovering that we've enabled our adult children not only because we love them, but because of deep-rooted emotional triggers that have almost nothing whatsoever to do with our adult children.

The same can be true for those of us dealing with any boundary-related issue. Because of our emotional triggers, our motives for not setting healthy boundaries in the first place are often false. Here are some examples.

- fear of loss of love or abandonment
- fear of others' anger
- fear of loneliness
- fear of losing the good me inside
- fear of consequences
- guilt
- fear of payback
- need for approval
- excessive identification with the other's loss

We do things because we feel guilty, need approval, or want revenge. We do things because other people deserve our help or because we're afraid they'll get mad if we don't. We do things because we don't want someone we love to experience pain or loss or because we fear being alone. Many women do things because they question their own competency and self-worth. It's impossible to list all our false motives, but they all stem from our need to love and be loved.

Some women would benefit from paying more attention to one emotion—righteous anger. When you've been passive and without boundaries for years, making a change can feel wrong. A certain degree of controlled righteous anger can help you to finally say you've had enough, the behavior must change, and a boundary must be set in place. Let this emotion work for you, not against you.

Looking for Love

Growing up, I saw how hard it was for my mom to raise three kids on her own. She was often lonely and frustrated, especially when she faced problems with money and housing. She cried a lot. I was convinced that Mom's loneliness, frustration, and fears were due to her need for a man to take care of her. I was sure that if she had a husband and we had a father who loved us, all would be right with the world.

Therefore, I vowed I was never going to be single. I was going to find a good man to love me and take care of me, one who would care deeply for me and our children. And we were going to own a house—no one was going to raise our rent and threaten to evict us. I began keeping my Mr. Right list very early in life so I wouldn't risk missing him when we met at last.

It was no surprise, then, that I dropped out of school after the ninth grade to run away and marry an 18-year-old Mr. Right. Except, of course, he wasn't. At age 15, I wasn't a very good judge of character. But this "man" represented security to me, and that's what mattered in my mind. I misinterpreted his obsessive need to control me as love and protection. The traits I initially saw as loving and warm quickly changed as I struggled for freedom. Our dangerous relationship soon became a painful prison. I now see how my damaged heart and soul skewed my perception of him.

The first time he hit me was shortly after we left the courthouse on the day we were married. In short order, he went from being the love of my life to my abuser, jailer, kidnapper, rapist, and attempted murderer. I spent a horrific year married to him—a sadistic man whose extreme physical and emotional abuse almost killed me. Becoming pregnant at 16 was a defining moment that suddenly made my reality crystal clear—I was now responsible for the life of an unborn child, and I had to keep this baby safe. Escaping with my life, I returned to live with my mother, where everything was fine as long as we didn't talk about it. And so we didn't.

Yet everything wasn't fine.

I had never been an overweight child, but I gained a staggering 100 pounds with my pregnancy. My focus at that time was staying alive and protecting my unborn child. My mother gave me shelter, and even though we moved several times to hide from this violent psychopath, he always managed to find us. Afraid to leave the house, I became reclusive, eating virtually from the time I woke up until I fell asleep. Food was the only comfort I could find. My mother only shook her head in sadness.

Every time I went to the clinic, I met with a different obstetrician, and I was in my ninth month when one of them finally connected the dots and read my chart, horrified that my weight had gone from 130 to 230 pounds in less than nine months.

I once read that every extra pound we carry on our bodies equals a pound of emotional pain we're carrying in our hearts. I believe it.

In retrospect, I now see that excess weight kept me safe. It protected me. Eating was the only way I could avoid addressing the truth because the truth was utterly impossible for me to articulate. I had no words for the emotions I was feeling, but inside I was screaming.

This was when my struggle with food and weight began. My relationship with food became one of the most destructive relationships I've ever known.

I was still looking for love, but another emotion was taking over—anger. It's one of the most powerful and potentially debilitating of the basic emotions. Using our anger against us is one of Satan's favorite tricks in his toolbox of bondage.

My anger percolated under the surface for years as I developed my dysfunctional enabling and codependent habits. Focusing on the needs of others and trying to "fix" them was much easier than identifying my true emotions and motivations and looking at the pain in my own life.

Can you relate in any way to this?

Ask yourself what you are afraid of and write down anything that comes to mind. The writing exercises I am giving you are intended to help you identify your true emotions and motivations. Sometimes we have to peel back many layers of emotions to find out what's really keeping us from taking control and walking in true spiritual authority.

The Angry Truth

Anger is something we feel. It exists for a reason and always deserves our respect and attention. We all have a right to everything we feel—and certainly our anger is no exception. In her *New York Times* bestselling book *The Dance of Anger*, Dr. Harriet Lerner has helped countless women find clarity, calm, and a voice in their most difficult relationships.

> Anger is a signal, and one worth listening to. Our anger may be a message that we are being hurt, that our rights are being violated, that our needs or wants are not being adequately met, or simply that something is not right. Our anger may tell us that we are not addressing an important emotional issue in our lives, or that too much of ourselves—our beliefs, values, desires, or ambitions—is being compromised in a relationship. Our anger may be a signal that we are doing more and giving more than we can comfortably do or give. Or our anger may warn us that others are doing too much for us, at the expense of our own competence

and growth. Just as physical pain tells us to take our hand off the hot stove, the pain of our anger preserves the very integrity of our self. Our anger can motivate us to say "no" to the ways in which we are defined by others and "yes" to the dictates of our inner self. [3]

Has anger been percolating in your heart? Write down ways that anger manifests itself in your life and your relationships.

The Motivation Behind the Madness

It takes courage to change. Sometimes, finding the courage to change means understanding why we do what we do—identifying the emotions that motivate us. So many components contribute to who we are today. The sad truth is, many of us have been so wrapped up in taking care of others, pleasing others at all cost, reacting to situations, and propelling the gerbil wheel that we've neglected to consider what may have fueled the fire of our chaotic lives in the first place.

- How did we get here?
- What makes us react as we do?
- Who are we under all of this responsibility and guilt?
- What really motivates us?

By the time I began to seriously ask myself those questions, I was well into my third decade of life. By then, I had developed some pretty unhealthy habits, including the way I enabled my adult son.

I loved my son and desired to help him, yet I was often motivated by fear, guilt, and anger. Fear of what would happen to him if I didn't come to his rescue. Guilt that I had been a poor parent and role model when he was a child. Anger at myself for not being able to "fix" my mess of a life. I was also angry at my ex-husband, who had betrayed my trust, broken my heart, and hurt me so deeply.

I know I'm not alone. Many women carry around those negative emotions and don't address them properly. Back then, it was all I could do to survive. Perhaps you can relate. But that was then, and this is now.

A.W. Tozer wrote, "It is doubtful whether God can bless a man greatly until He has hurt him deeply."

Many women who find it hard to set boundaries have been hurt deeply. It's time to process the hurts and claim the blessings.

I know how hard it can be to shine the light on your emotions and motives. However, you need to be aware that everything you have experienced in life is connected, making you the person you are today. A person God loves and values. A person who is worthy of having her needs met.

What are the most significant hurts you can recall? Write them in your notebook. This may be a surprisingly difficult and painful exercise. If that is the case, stop and pick up your Bible and randomly open it. Read both the left and right pages and ask God to speak to you in any way He chooses. Trust Him to lead you where He wants you to go.

What Do We Need?

Our emotions shape our needs, goals, and desires—the things that motivate us.

Sometimes we ignore our emotions and needs by burying them under an unhealthy focus on other people, places, and things—including food, which I address in *Setting Boundaries® with Food*.

> Listening to the hunger causes us to ask what it is we're really craving. Understanding? Love? Acceptance? What emotions are welling up in us when our first instinct is to push them back down with food? Fear? Anger? Worry? Many of us have been hiding our true emotions and needs for so long we haven't got a clue what they are. Remember, we have three primary needs: love, significance, and security. [4]

How about you? Are you even aware of your needs? If so, are those needs being compromised, ignored, or violated?

Psychologist Abraham Maslow introduced his concept of a hierarchy of needs in his 1943 paper "A Theory of Human Motivation" and his subsequent book *Motivation and Personality*. His hierarchy of needs is most often displayed as a pyramid, with number one on the list at the bottom of the pyramid—our most basic need. This hierarchy suggests that people are motivated to fulfill basic needs before moving on to other needs.

Use your notebook and make five columns, and number them one through five. Then write down how your needs are being met (or not) in each column.

1. physiological—breathing, food, water, and sleep
2. safety—security of body, employment, resources, morality, family, health, and property
3. love and belonging—friendship, family, sexual intimacy
4. esteem—self-esteem, self-respect, confidence, achievement, respect of others, respect by others
5. self-actualization—morality, creativity, spontaneity, problem solving, lack of prejudice, acceptance of facts

For all the information available at our fingertips, many of us don't quite reach levels four and five. Or if we do, we don't spend much time there because of the misconception that it's not the Christian thing to do—as though seeking a better understanding of who we are and what we need keeps us from trusting God and His infinite plan for our lives.

How can we possibly set healthy boundaries if we don't know what we need?

In addition to Maslow's list of the five basic needs that motivate us, other factors drive us as well. Review the list below and ask God to reveal areas that you are either ignoring or focusing on too much. Write about these needs in your notebook.

- acceptance—the need for approval
- independence—the need for individuality and competence

- order—the need for organized, stable, predictable environments
- physical activity—the need for exercise
- power—the need for influence
- social contact—the need for friends
- status—the need to belong
- tranquility—the need to be safe

Break the Chain

Identifying our needs is crucial even though we must occasionally place those needs on the back burner or even sacrifice them for a season. If you are consistently ignoring your emotions and needs, then your feelings of depression, self-destruction, or despair are likely to increase. Something is wrong. It's time to get help.

A host of psychological terms are associated with our motivations, or the reasons why we do the things we do. One of those terms was coined by Sigmund Freud—*repetition compulsion*. Of course, we're far more than labels and jargon, yet in my experience talking to countless individuals about boundaries, I've found repetition compulsion to be alive, well, and thriving. Some families have been repeating the same behavior and expecting different results for generations.

If this is true in your family, God can use you to break that chain. He can use you to set a new example and build a new bridge of communication, starting with the change in your own heart.

We can begin by asking the Holy Spirit to help us identify and understand our emotions, motivations, and needs. Are we giving to others out of authentic love, compassion, honesty, and respect, or from places of guilt, fear, resentment, anger, and bondage? Is what we are doing helping the people we care about, or is it hurting them? Are our own needs being met? Exploring our emotions and discovering what motivates us can free us from the bondage of poor boundary choices.

We have seen that we need to consider other people's personalities and emotions as well as our own. The same is true with motivations. What motivates that person to act the way he or she does? If the person is your own child, you may be aware of some of the influences in his or her life. An absent father may have left the child feeling rejected. That could motivate certain types of behavior when the child becomes a teen or an adult. For example, an uncommunicative husband may have been rejected as a child.

Keep in mind that some children who were physically or sexually abused grow up to be abusers themselves. Victims of sexual abuse may also develop unhealthy attitudes toward sexual intimacy. As you consider the challenging people in your life, always take time to consider the reasons why they may act the way they do. These are not excuses for their inappropriate behavior, but they can help us clarify what is happening and know how to implement more effective boundaries in the future.

Of course, not all of those with whom we need to set boundaries are close to us. We usually can't know why a coworker is the way she is or why the next-door neighbor does the things she does. In every case, however, we can work with what we know and try to be loving but firm. The key is to understand that just like us, everyone has a backstory, and everyone is precious in God's eyes.

As you learn about your own personality, emotions, and motivations and apply the SANITY Steps to your daily life, ask God to empower you to respond in a kinder and gentler way when challenging people pull your emotional trigger. Be intentional about this request. And remember, you may be the only face of God a person will see.

Our culture loves to restore things. We restore old cars, houses, furniture, and even wedding dresses. We take something old and make it new again, sometimes even increasing its original value.

God restores us the same way. And sometimes He sends us as His ambassadors to help Him restore others, even as we ourselves are being restored.

Peace, Not Passivity

I remember a conversation I had with a woman who had lost her husband and was facing serious health and financial issues. Somehow she had maintained an aura of peace around her. She described how God was using a current Bible study to fill her heart and help change her pattern of thinking. "My situation hasn't changed at all," she said. "In fact, in many ways it's getting worse. But when I decided to take control and not let my circumstances control me, God began to give me revelation after revelation. As I read my Bible, I began to see how much I was being controlled by fear and how wrong that motivation was!"

Being controlled by other people's negative behavior, bad habits, or external influence is no way to live an authentic life.

The only way we can find peace is to depend on God, put our trust in Him, and pray for the wisdom and discernment we need to take control of the things we *can* control—the things God wants us to control in order to fulfill His purpose for our lives.

When we're uncertain about where to start, the well-known Serenity Prayer is a good place to begin. The Serenity Prayer is the common name for an originally untitled prayer by the theologian Reinhold Niebuhr. It has been adopted by Alcoholics Anonymous and other 12-step programs. This part of the prayer is quoted most often:

God, grant me the serenity to accept the things I cannot change, courage to change the things I can, and wisdom to know the difference.

Learning to Control What We Can

In *Setting Boundaries® with Your Adult Children*, I explained that parents who enable their children have often circumvented those children's natural growth. In our honest desire to shield our children from harm, we have discouraged them from accepting the consequences of their actions—from learning valuable life-lessons from their choices. Instead of helping our kids, we have handicapped them.

Many of us have done the same thing to ourselves. In our honest desire to be good Christian women, many of us have confused taking control with being controlling. We have spent years living less than authentic lives, confused about our roles and responsibilities, uncertain about our identity, fearful of rejection, and bogged down by guilt. Many of us haven't fully understood or experienced the consequences of our actions. We've handicapped ourselves.

When we have weak, nonexistent, or violated boundaries, we lack peace in our lives. Life can be extremely stressful when we consistently run on the gerbil wheel of insanity as a result of our choices.

We've prohibited ourselves from being all we can be and all God wants us to be. We've sacrificed our peace.

It's time to stop.

God's Word instructs us to look at the choices we're making. "Let's take a good look at the way we're living and reorder our lives under God" (Lamentations 3:40 MSG).

Is it time to reorder your life? If so, I've got a great tool to help. The weekly recitation of the SANITY Support Creed is a critical component in the 12-week program to help parents break negative habits and set healthy boundaries with their adult children. I've revised that creed for women who want to jump off the gerbil wheel of insanity they have perpetuated. It appears in appendix 1 at the end of the book. I encourage you to photocopy it and recite it daily.

Lack of Peace Can Destroy Us

I first noticed Elizabeth about halfway through my talk when the woman sitting next to her handed her a tissue to wipe the tears coursing down her cheeks.

I enjoy making an audience laugh, but I'm much more concerned about what makes them cry. It's often through the shedding of tears that God is able to do the work He wants to do. Clearly, God was at work in Elizabeth.

I later found out she was divorced and raising her oldest daughter's three-year-old child. The daughter was unmarried, pregnant with her second child, and living with a man who didn't want the responsibility of raising children.

Elizabeth also had two adult sons who lived with her. One was developmentally disabled, and the other was a raging alcoholic who punched holes in the walls and broke things when he was drunk, which was often.

Elizabeth worked full-time as a cashier at a big-box store and had recently taken a part-time job from home as a telemarketer, which allowed her to care for her granddaughter and disabled son. She had clearly reached the end of her rope long before I met her, but she had developed many excuses to keep running on the gerbil wheel of insanity.

God spoke directly to her when I shared my story and then pointed my mommy finger of authority at the audience and said, "Enabling is not helping, ladies, and you will never find peace until you're ready, willing, and able to see the part you're playing in the dysfunctional drama."

An old Danish proverb says, "What you are is God's gift to you; what you do with yourself is your gift to God."

After tearfully sharing her story with me, she said, "I'm not sure how much more of this I can take. I'm just so tired...I just want peace in my life."

An old Danish proverb says, "What you are is God's gift to you; what you do with yourself is your gift to God."

What Elizabeth was doing with herself was slow and steady suicide by insanity—certainly not the kind of gift God had in mind. This was not how God intended for her to live.

> Finding any kind of peace in life will be virtually impossible if we don't see our value and worth in God's eyes.

The Peace of Identity

Finding any kind of peace in life will be virtually impossible if we don't see our value and worth in God's eyes. The Bible says, "See what great love the Father has lavished on us, that we should be called the children of God!" (1 John 3:1). We will never be without the love and compassion of the Lord. We deny our identity in Christ when we allow ourselves to be abused, mistreated, or subjugated and when we neglect to see ourselves through God's eyes.

What caused Elizabeth to think she deserved this kind of treatment? That she was really helping the players in this dysfunctional drama? How were her negative emotions driving her? What were her motivations? She was on the verge of a nervous breakdown when I met her, and if she truly wanted to find peace, she needed to make some serious changes by taking control of her life and setting appropriate boundaries.

Finding peace isn't a passive exercise, especially when we've traveled so far from God's plan and purpose for our lives.

It took me years to jump off the gerbil wheel of people-pleasing insanity—to realize that my first responsibility was to please God, to understand that my sinful nature would forever be in battle with my new life in Christ, and to know that because of His gift of free will, I would always be responsible to choose whether to obey Him, depend on Him, and have faith and trust in Him.

When our actions and attitudes please God, a sense of peace will ultimately follow. Ask yourself if your actions and attitudes are pleasing God.

During my first years as a new believer, I found myself saying yes to virtually everything I was asked to do in any ministry outreach. Back then, I was working full-time as a professional fund-raiser and was experienced in nonprofit development and public relations. I conducted strategic planning for director boards and advisory committees, and I assisted in capital campaigns that raised millions of dollars. I thought of myself as a church volunteer dropped from heaven, as if I had been sent from God to save them.

Yeah, right.

Actually, I *was* sent by God, that was certain. But *not* so I could be anyone's savior. God was teaching me a lesson from Isaiah 5:21: "Woe to those who are wise in their own eyes and clever in their own sight."

Truthfully, I wanted so much to please these people *and* to please God. Unfortunately, in my seriously distorted understanding, I thought that blindly saying yes to everything asked of me was saying yes to God.

Alas, that was not the case, especially when I would overcommit and let someone down. After all, there are only so many hours in a day.

As a chronic enabler with a choleric personality temperament and a past history of abuse, I easily fell into negative patterns of response that directly opposed obedience to God's Word. Desperate to please, I dove into every project headfirst before ascertaining the depth of the water.

To reorder my life, I had to stop looking to others to affirm my purpose, bring me security, and fill the empty places in my soul that only God could fill. I first had to deal with my past so I could begin making healthy choices in my present.

Such was the case with Elizabeth as well. Her current choices were tied to deep feelings of insecurity she had acquired as a young girl.

In her book *The Secrets Women Keep: What Women Hide and the Truth That Brings Them Freedom,* Dr. Jill Hubbard convincingly argues that it will be difficult to ever find peace in our lives when we are hiding secrets.

> A secret is a part of ourselves we're keeping hidden in darkness, but it cries out for the light. We know instinctively that we can't flourish in the dark, so as long as we are hiding pieces of our truth from the light, we experience a disturbance in our hearts and souls. It might be subtle, like an undercurrent of feeling that something's not right. Or it might be overwhelming, determining the shape of our relationships and our lives.

> When we are going through life acting as one person on the outside, while we're really a different person on the inside, we can't have peace. We know something's off. There's an acute sense of dissonance when our interiors and exteriors don't match.[1]

She also writes,

> A surprising number of families keep the peace by hiding or ignoring huge pieces of their reality. Keeping the secret serves everyone. Well, at least all the adults. The desire for some people to create the picture of the life they want by erasing the mistakes can be very strong. We tend to cover up messiness so we can present our lives as neat and tidy."[2]

Is your life neat and tidy? Or is the exhaustion that comes when you try to "cover up messiness" sapping the energy from your life? Where are you getting your power to survive?

The Peace of Power

I spend the majority of my days on the computer. I use a wireless mouse, and eventually the batteries in it begin to lose power. I can always tell when it's happening because the cursor sometimes doesn't scroll properly. Sometimes I resort to holding the mouse a little more tightly, pressing it into the mouse pad a little harder, or even shaking it and pounding it on my desktop—as if that's going to help. In most cases, all I need to do is stop long enough to take the back off the mouse and change the batteries. In fact, an automatic prompt informs me that my batteries are running low. I usually ignore that until the last possible moment.

What prompts do we receive when our physical, emotional, or spiritual batteries start to run low? What happens when we try to operate on depleted batteries? Whom do we depend on to help us find the peace and sanity that will refresh our spirits? The Bible says, "You, LORD, keep my lamp burning; my God turns my darkness into light" (Psalm 18:28). Our power comes from the Almighty, as the Bible says. "God has spoken plainly, and I have heard it many times: Power, O God, belongs to you" (Psalm 62:11 NLT). When we understand our identity and we access God's power, we find peace.

A Christian without peace is like a wireless mouse without batteries—totally ineffective.

We must take responsibility for recharging our own batteries, or we won't be good to anyone, including God. The Bible says, "You will keep in perfect peace those whose minds are steadfast, because they trust in you. Trust in the LORD forever, for the LORD, the LORD himself, is the Rock eternal" (Isaiah 26:3-4).

The Peace of Protection

I remember reading *Wonder Woman* comic books as a young girl and then later watching *The New Adventures of Wonder Woman* on television, starring the indestructible and beautiful Lynda Carter. I loved that she could be two people and possess two entirely different personae. Besides, she had some rather nifty superpowers and magical tools, including the Lasso of Truth and a stunning golden tiara. And who could forget those fabulous bulletproof bracelets?

I was enthralled by the power Wonder Woman commanded and the self-confidence Diana Prince (her alter ego) exuded. My dream wasn't to grow up and become a cartoon or TV superhero. I just wanted to be as brave and fearless as she was. I wanted to be powerful so I could feel protected, safe, significant, and loved.

I had never felt safe or protected in my childhood. I grew up without an earthly father, and I was completely unaware that I had a heavenly Father.

It's hard to put into words the overwhelming sense of protection I felt when I met the Lord and asked Him into my heart. My journey since then has included plenty of trials and tribulations, but it has been void of the emptiness I once felt as a fatherless girl—the emptiness many women feel today.

When we have a relationship with God, we can rest assured we will never be abandoned or alone. We will always have a home in God's heart. I know that in God's eyes, I am His child forever. And this security brings me peace.

> For Christ himself has brought peace to us. He united Jews and Gentiles into one people when, in his own body on the cross, he broke down the wall of hostility that separated us. He did this by ending the system of law with its commandments and regulations. He made peace between Jews and Gentiles by creating in himself one new people from the two groups. Together as one body, Christ reconciled both groups to God by means of his death on the cross, and our hostility toward each other was put to death.
>
> He brought this Good News of peace to you Gentiles who were far away from him, and peace to the Jews who were

near. Now all of us can come to the Father through the same Holy Spirit because of what Christ has done for us (Ephesians 2:14-18 NLT).

<hr/>

Peace can be ours when we...

- are walking in God's will
- trust in the Lord
- understand our spiritual worth and identity in Christ
- stop looking to others to affirm our value, identity, and sense of purpose
- serve God out of joy and deep gratitude
- serve others from an authentic place of love
- understand God's plan and purpose for our lives

<hr/>

The Peace of Purpose

Nothing in our lives is arbitrary. God never does anything accidently, and it isn't a mere coincidence that you are here in this place today. The Bible says, "The LORD will work out his plans for my life" (Psalm 138:8 NLT). We have been created to do good works for God, and He has already prepared fulfilling and meaningful work for us to do.

God reveals His plan and purpose for our lives in various ways, including through the things we've experienced and the lessons we've learned. Just as we're changing our perspective on control, so too must we change our perspective on the pain from our past. There are no accidents in God's kingdom.

If you aren't certain about God's plan and purpose, ask Him to reveal it to you. Pray every day for your eyes and heart to be opened in a new and fresh way so that you may serve God authentically.

We can expect a new level of peace to come into our lives when we begin to change our perspective on control and use the SANITY Steps to set boundaries. This doesn't mean life won't have its share of challenges. However, when you ask God to reveal His plan and purpose for you, when you humbly present your requests to God, "the peace of God, which transcends all understanding, will guard your hearts and your minds in Christ Jesus" (Philippians 4:7).

The Prince of Peace

Shortly before Jesus' crucifixion, He said to His disciples, "Peace I leave with you; my peace I give you. I do not give to you as the world gives. Do not let your hearts be troubled and do not be afraid" (John 14:27). A little later, He told them, "I have told you these things, so that in me you may have peace. In this world you will have trouble. But take heart! I have overcome the world" (John 16:33).

After His resurrection, Jesus appeared again to His disciples, and His first words were simple but powerful.

> "Peace be with you!"…The disciples were overjoyed when they saw the Lord.
>
> Again Jesus said, "Peace be with you!"…
>
> A week later his disciples were in the house again, and Thomas was with them. Though the doors were locked, Jesus came and stood among them and said, "Peace be with you!" (John 20:19-21,26).

Clearly, Jesus earnestly wanted His disciples to have peace. And just as earnestly, He wants all God's children to experience the supernatural fullness of peace that comes when we have an intimate relationship with Him. "The fruit of that righteousness will be peace; its effect will be quietness and confidence forever" (Isaiah 32:17).

However, our enemy, Satan, doesn't want us to live supernatural lives. He doesn't want us to experience miracles when we need miracles. He doesn't want us to experience God's presence in our lives. He doesn't want us to have peace, and he will do just about anything to keep us caught up in chaotic emotions and situations. The evil one doesn't want us to walk in power, purpose, or protection.

But the enemy can't win. "With God we will gain the victory, and he will trample down our enemies" (Psalm 60:12).

Finding peace in a life without boundaries is difficult. Finding peace in a life without the Lord is impossible.

> Consider the blameless, observe the upright; a future awaits those who seek peace (Psalm 37:37).

The Fruit of Healthy Boundaries

Implementing a boundary is like sowing a seed. We plant the seed, expecting a good harvest. We set a boundary in place, hoping for a fruitful result. We hope to address these issues that keep us from moving ahead in our relationship with God and the fulfillment of His plan.

The apostle Paul understood the correlation between being in right relationship with God and producing a bountiful harvest, as he shared in his letter to the Christians in Colossae.

> The fruit of healthy boundaries includes healthy relationships with ourselves, with others, and most importantly, with the One who created us.

> We have not stopped praying for you since we first heard about you. We ask God to give you complete knowledge of his will and to give you spiritual wisdom and understanding. Then the way you live will always honor and please the Lord, and your lives will produce every kind of good fruit. All the while, you will grow as you learn to know God better and better (Colossians 1:9-10 NLT).

The fruits of healthy boundaries include healthy relationships with ourselves, with others, and most importantly, with the One who created us. When the desire of our heart is to love God and allow that love to flow unobstructed through us and out into the world, our lives change.

Remember the admonition in Proverbs 4:23 to guard your heart? When we begin to live a life that is *not* governed by emotional drama, chaos, and crisis (these are direct results of weak or nonexistent boundaries), we begin to walk with a strength of power and purpose that changes who we are. When the roots of our lives sink deeply into God's Word and His will, we change. It all begins on the inside.

> God wants to use us to make a difference in the lives of our family and friends.

In her book *The Truth Principle*, Leslie Vernick speaks of how our loving God changes us from the inside out.

> The process of personal growth, Christian maturity, fruitfulness, and becoming more and more like Christ begins with seeds of love sown in our heart. Christ often used the metaphor of garden life as a teaching tool. An apple tree cannot bear figs, can it? Why not? Because the very essence of the apple tree is defined by its roots, which are apple-tree roots and not fig-tree roots. Apples are a natural outgrowth of the roots. We will never have Christlikeness or the fruit of the Spirit in our lives if our roots are shallow, underdeveloped, diseased, or of a different stock.
>
> What are the roots of Christian living? The roots are love. Jesus tells us that we cannot bear fruit unless we are rooted in Him (John 15). Just as a branch is in essence and nature like the vine from which it sprouts, we are to reflect God's image in us, and God is love. He tells us that when we love him we will obey him. Rules don't bring heart obedience, but love does.[1]

God wants to use us to make a difference in the lives of our family and friends. He wants us to bear fruit, to make our choices based on biblical truth, to love Him, and to love all people. Loving all people is very difficult—especially people who are violating our boundaries. Proper boundaries can actually enhance our ability to love and respect others and help them to love and respect us. The lack of boundaries can promote dissension and resentment.

We met Elizabeth in chapter 11. She loved her son, but she could no longer condone his drinking. She knew he needed help, but he refused to get help, and she couldn't force him to reach out for it. However, she could set some firm boundaries regarding acceptable behavior in her own home. Fortunately, Elizabeth was willing to *Assemble Supportive People* around her (the "A" Step in SANITY) and trust the wise counsel she received from these godly men and women. She felt convicted the time was right to make critical changes, and with the help of her SANITY Support Group, she was able to develop and *Implement an Action Plan* (The "I" Step in SANITY), which outlined the steps to effectively address her adult son's alcoholism and increasingly violent behavior.

Her plan also included a written document for her son that defined her new boundaries concerning intoxication, destruction of property, and physical and verbal abuse. It included specific consequences for crossing the boundaries.

Most written action plans are developed for our eyes only and are intended to help us stay on track with our own goals. However, sometimes we should present someone with a written document that clarifies the new boundaries, or in this case, the new house rules. (Details for developing a plan of action appear in appendix 2.)

Elizabeth presented this document to her son, and within a few months he moved out of her house.

This wasn't an easy process, and the months before his move were filled with trauma and tears as Elizabeth consistently enforced the consequences she had established, including calling the police when her son locked himself in his bedroom and proceeded to destroy the furniture. This time, she was going to say what she meant and mean what she said.

Unhealthy Relationships Cannot Produce Fruit

Boundary violations can take place in any unhealthy relationship. People may consistently use you to serve their needs, take advantage of your good nature and your desire to please, or contribute to your poor self-worth by negativity, criticism, or other unhealthy attitudes and behaviors that diminish your ability to produce fruit.

Elizabeth was accepting unacceptable behavior from her adult son and daughter. She was enabling the wrong behavior and sometimes even funding it. This was not God's will for her life or for the lives of her children.

Author June Hunt identifies characteristics of health and unhealthy relationships.

> If you look closely, you can evaluate the health of any relationship by seeing the type of fruit it produces—whether the fruit is good or bad. Jesus said, "A good tree cannot bear bad fruit, and a bad tree cannot bear good fruit. Every tree that does not bear good fruit is cut down and thrown into the fire. Thus, by their fruit you will recognize them" (Matthew 7:18-20 NIV).[2]

Ask yourself if your relationships are bearing good fruit. Look at them individually. Are you a better person for being in this relationship? Is the other person better for having known you? Are you living your fullest potential and walking in God's plan and purpose? Or has your inability to set healthy boundaries and take appropriate control left you unfruitful? Is it time for some serious pruning?

> When our relationships lack healthy boundaries and are out of priority, is it any wonder our lives are not producing a bountiful harvest of fruit?

God, Why Aren't You Using Me?

Henry Blackaby writes, "If you are experiencing a time of fruitlessness right now, you may be trying to do things on your own that God has not initiated."[3]

When our relationships lack healthy boundaries and are out of priority, is it any wonder our lives are not producing a bountiful harvest of fruit?

Looking at boundary-related issues in our lives through this lens of bearing fruit can change our perspective on life. Many of us have been trying to ignore our relationship problems for years. We were bearing nothing but bad fruit, and we didn't even realize it.

> I pray for you constantly, asking God, the glorious Father of our Lord Jesus Christ, to give you spiritual wisdom and insight so that you might grow in your knowledge of God. I pray that your hearts will be flooded with light so that you can understand the confident hope he has given to those he called—his holy people who are his rich and glorious inheritance (Ephesians 1:16-18 NLT).

We are not likely to slide into negative self-talk or self-defeating habits when we truly know that each of us is a daughter of the King with a divine birthright and an incomparable identity. When we know our identity, we find the strength and wisdom we need to set healthy boundaries and to walk in ways that produce fruit. June Hunt touches on this in her book *Seeing Yourself Through God's Eyes*.

> As we grow stronger in our faith, obedience, and identity, we will begin to flourish in ways we could never have imaged.

> Every person born into this world has had difficulty with identity at some time or another. All of us have struggled with our self-image.

> Many spend a lifetime manipulating acceptance and attention from others, thinking they are building an indestructible tower of self-worth. Yet when people fail us and our logical expectations of our loved ones fall painfully short, our own self-worth can begin to crumble.

> That's exactly the problem if we let our *identity be in another*

person—we give that person too much control of us. And more so, we miss the vision God has of us and the immense value He places on us. The steps to understanding these truths are paved throughout Scripture. To tread these steps, we need to have a full understanding of what is meant by *identity*.

Have you ever asked yourself, *Who am I? Where am I going?* Do you understand your God-given worth? How essential to have accurate answers to these questions so that you can be what God created you to be and do what God created you to do.[4]

Bearing the Fruit of SANITY

As we grow stronger in our faith, obedience, and identity, we will begin to flourish in ways we could never have imaged. When we make the choice to exercise control over ourselves and claim the spiritual authority Jesus has given us, we can influence and change our world.

When Elizabeth began to accept responsibility for the part she played in the dysfunction in her family and to make intentional decisions to walk in spiritual authority and SANITY, her life began to change dramatically.

Likewise for Susan when she finally met with her boss to discuss her workload and began to spend more time with her husband and celebrate his retirement and their new life.

The Bible says, "The righteous will flourish like a palm tree, they will grow like a cedar of Lebanon; planted in the house of the LORD, they will flourish in the courts of our God. They will still bear fruit in old age, they will stay fresh and green, proclaiming, 'The LORD is upright; he is my Rock, and there is no wickedness in him'" (Psalm 92:12-15).

Sometimes our inability to establish healthy boundaries with difficult people or situations affects innocent parties around us. They become collateral damage. Conversely, when we change, their lives may change as well.

With his violent older brother out of the house, Elizabeth's disabled son began to flourish in amazing ways. As she began to set firm and loving boundaries with him, his self-worth increased, and he began to take on more appropriate responsibilities. He is currently taking a class at a local community college and exploring assisted-living programs. Additionally, to protect the safety of her granddaughter, Elizabeth is in the process of gaining legal custody, a decision that came after a great deal of prayer and communication with her daughter and the Department of Child Protective Services. Many changes are going on in her world.

"My life is far from idyllic," she says. "And I know it sounds odd, but I feel strangely at peace. I wish I could say my eldest son was sober. That isn't the case, but I continue to pray for him. I know what I did was right when I finally took control of my chaotic life. I'm only sorry I didn't do it sooner. I'm not sure what the future will bring, but I do know that God will see me through it."

God is also seeing Elizabeth through her final exams at cosmetology school.

"I'm the oldest person in my class, but this is something I always wanted to do. I really think this is what God wants me to do. I can hardly believe I'm actually doing it. I thank God every day that I was able to find SANITY."

What Fruit Is Your Life Bearing?

As we learn how to take control with God at the helm, we can learn how to respond to unhealthy behavior and attitudes in a positive, firm, and loving manner. This change in our own behavior and attitude can transform our lives and the lives of those around us. As our spiritual authority grows, we will be convicted (provoked) to act in ways we feel God is calling us.

Pastor Tony Evans often says, "Every person has a garden where God has planted us. He expects us to reign over our garden. He calls us to exercise rule over our space and to bear fruit."

Our personal garden includes our family, community, church, job, and any other area where God calls us.

My pastor recently shared a story about his family doctor, a man whose faith consistently increased over the years as he prayed to walk in God's will. As the roots of his faith grew deeper, and as he began to exercise more spiritual authority, he felt God calling him into politics. Within a few years, his garden expanded from the community to the country. Today, that family doctor serves as a United States senator.

Where is your garden? In what area has God planted you to carry out His plan and purpose?

The Bible says, "You are the light of the world. A town built on a hill cannot be hidden. Neither do people light a lamp and put it under a bowl. Instead they put it on its stand, and it gives light to everyone in the house. In the same way, let your light shine before others, that they may see your good deeds and glorify your Father in heaven" (Matthew 5:14-16).

What would you be doing if your life wasn't caught up in a drama of dysfunction caused by a lack of healthy boundaries? How could God be using you, your gifts, and your abilities more effectively? What fruit would your life produce if you were able to successfully dismantle the gerbil wheel of insanity? Take the time to stop and pray about these questions and record your thoughts in your notebook.

We set healthy boundaries and pursue SANITY because we want to live fruitful lives. We want to claim the resurrection power and spiritual authority of Jesus and to use that power to change and transform our lives and the lives of others. We want to walk in truth and stand in victory.

How to Walk in God's Authority

In a powerful Easter message, Pastor Chuck Angel began a sermon series titled Seven Secrets of Spiritual Authority Learned from the Jewish Kings. The first Jewish King he considered was Jesus Christ.

Pastor Chuck has graciously allowed me to share his Three Tips to Walk in God's Authority, tips that will enable us to say goodbye to insanity and embrace sanity with uncompromising command and control. Applying the SANITY Steps in conjunction with the three authoritative tips below can equip us with a supernatural power that can change our lives.

Three Tips to Walk in God's Authority

1. Affirm the truth that the power present in you is more powerful than what opposes you.
2. Present yourself as a living sacrifice.
3. Walk in your authority with confidence.

1. Affirm the truth that the power present in you is more powerful than what opposes you.

First John 4:4 says, "You, dear children, are from God and have overcome them, because the one who is in you is greater than the one who is in the world."

Regardless of the experience we are facing, it is imperative that we walk with the assurance that our God is awesome and powerful. We can do all things through Him, including authentically saying yes and graciously saying no.

2. Present yourself as a living sacrifice.

Romans 12:1 says, "Therefore, I urge you, brothers and sisters, in view of God's mercy, to offer your bodies as a living sacrifice, holy and pleasing to God—this is your true and proper worship."

To help us ponder the full meaning of this tip, Pastor Chuck said, "This takes a willingness to be obedient because a living sacrifice can crawl off the altar." In other words, this step isn't always easy.

Likewise, when we jump off the gerbil wheel of insanity, we sacrifice our own negative behavior and our own excuses for why we have made the choices we've made, including the habits, attitudes, and choices that have kept us from *Yielding Everything to God* (the "Y" Step in SANITY). Just as our walk with the Lord requires a willingness to be obedient, so too does our commitment to choose SANITY.

Regardless of the roadblocks we face in life, even when things get really tough, we must vow to hang on to Jesus and not crawl off the altar of salvation and power.

3. Walk in your authority with confidence.

As followers of Jesus we have access to His overcoming power. Christianity is not just religious rules and regulations, it's a life characterized by the power and spiritual authority God has given us. Taking control and claiming this power on a daily basis is really the foundation of the SANITY Steps.

When we walk with confidence and not in arrogance, God can use us in mighty ways.

When we address the difficult issues in our lives through the lenses of faith and the desire to serve God, we can position ourselves not only to receive the full measure of God's blessing for our lives but also to be blessings to others.

The road we walk to set healthy boundaries, take control, and find SANITY will give us life experience and wisdom we can share with others in our home, workplace, church, or ministry.

Go Forth and Bear Fruit!

God saved us to serve Him. He wants us to be free in Christ, not to remain in bondage to the feelings of guilt, anger, and fear that the enemy uses to keep us from being powerful and effective women. The Bible says, "The one who does what is sinful is of the devil, because the devil has been sinning from the beginning. The reason the Son of God appeared was to destroy the devil's work" (1 John 3:8).

And He has called us to help Him do that.

However, as author Jill Briscoe reminds us, "The forces of evil have invaded the forces of good in our world today. We are at war. It is God's war. Souls are at stake. Christ is our Commander, and we men and women are His soldiers." [5]

It's up to each of us to use the brains God gave us to be effective players in the game of life! I often say that during my years as a New Age believer I was so open-minded that my brain slipped out. I know I wasn't alone.

Thankfully, as a Christian woman, I regained my brain. I discovered that finding SANITY involves more than setting healthy boundaries. It puts us in a state of mind and a place of peace where we can claim the power and spiritual authority of Christ. Through a renewed mind and protected heart, we can sink our roots of love deeper and deeper, enabling us to bear fruit that will bring honor and glory to God's kingdom.

Remember, peace isn't passive. Renewing our mind and protecting our hearts isn't passive. The journey to peace and sanity isn't an e-ticket to an easy ride. Rather, we're no longer at war with the One who is in charge. We're ready to walk boldly in God's authority and to let God use us in remarkable ways.

However, as the righteous begin to flourish, we must be prepared. Pastor Chuck Angel says, "When we take ground for Jesus Christ, all hell will break loose. We will feel the heat. And the hotter it gets, the more certain we can be that we are on the right track."

Pastor Chuck highlights three secrets to remember as we strive to walk in spiritual authority. These secrets will help us as the heat gets turned up.

1. Understand the overcoming power of Jesus Christ.

2. Be heart smart (guard your heart, as Proverbs 4:23 says).

3. Gain strength from the help of wise counsel.

We're living in a world and a time unlike any other in history. The lines between right and wrong are not as blurred as they have been in the past several decades. Christian women are beginning to take a stand, to speak up about what they feel is right. We are no longer willing to sit quietly on the sidelines.

How is God preparing you and your garden?

The kingdom needs more Deborah disciples! It's time for us to produce the fruit of healthy boundaries and SANITY and to let God use us in battle.

It's time to go for it, girl!

Go for It, Girl!

You're almost there!

You know what to do, and I'm confident you'll do it. The results will be up to God, and He will be with you as you navigate this new course and decide what comes next.

Without a doubt, the inability to set healthy boundaries with the people, places, and things in our lives that keep us from walking in right relationship with the Lord is a challenge for women everywhere. However, SANITY is possible, and I pray you have found it here.

Our Primary Call

We should step back for a moment and remind ourselves again that each of us is called to a personal relationship with God through Jesus Christ. Everything follows from this. The fruit of our relationship with Christ moves us to fulfill our calling in work. That work—whether serving on the mission field or delivering mail—is a holy calling of God.

God holds a high view of work because He created each person in His image and for an express purpose that we might reflect His glory in all aspects of life. "And whatever you do, whether in word or deed, do it all in the name of the Lord Jesus, giving thanks to God the Father through him" (Colossians 3:17).

Looking prayerfully at the life of Jesus helped me learn more about boundaries. As I read my Bible, I discovered that Jesus set boundaries repeatedly. He was truly the author of sanity.

I discovered that in His humanity, Jesus had limitations that He accepted in a relaxed way. He had a human body that needed nourishment and rest and could be in only one place at a time. He had only 24 hours in a day regardless of how many things He would have liked to accomplish.

Jesus occasionally prioritized His own needs over the needs of other people, and He did so without feeling guilty. His personal soul care included separating Himself from people to be alone with God, whom He called Abba, or Papa. Jesus lived in a rhythm of life that kept Him free from insanity. And even far beyond that, it kept Him full of God, full of grace and truth, and therefore ready and able to compassionately and generously respond to people's needs and crises.

Unlike many devoted servants of the Lord, Jesus didn't live on the defensive, overextending Himself, getting increasingly tired, and then finally taking a break (or having a breakdown). Instead, Jesus lived on the offensive against temptation and Satan. He was proactive, consistently investing in His intimate relationship with His Father, and this gave Him energy and focus. Jesus lived by the principle that life begins with the first step in SANITY, in stopping and being still, so He was never in danger of hopping on the gerbil wheel of insanity.

As I read about Jesus' life, I also discovered that Jesus wasn't always nice to people. He wasn't a people pleaser. Often He didn't do what people wanted Him to do. There were many people He didn't help. And whenever He did help people, He expected them to do their part. For instance, even in Jesus' miracles, He asked people to do something—usually something they felt they couldn't do. For example, the blind man had to walk a long way to the pool of Siloam to wash the mud out of his eyes.

These understandings about Jesus' way of life convinced me that it was good and right for me to learn how to say no to people, speak the truth in love, and live within my personal limitations.

Jesus Taught Us Examples of How to Set Boundaries

Pray. "When you pray, go into your room, close the door and pray to your Father, who is unseen" (Matthew 6:6).

Be honest and direct. Don't pressure people or try to get them to do things. "All you need to say is simply 'Yes' or 'No'; anything beyond this comes from the evil one" (Matthew 5:37).

Set priorities. "No one can serve two masters. Either you will hate the one and love the other, or you will be devoted to the one and despise the other" (Luke 16:13).

Please God, not people. "How can you believe since you accept glory from one another but do not seek the glory that comes from the only God?" (John 5:44).

Obey God. "'What do you think? There was a man who had two sons. He went to the first and said, "Son, go and work today in the vineyard."

"'"I will not," he answered, but later he changed his mind and went.

"'Then the father went to the other son and said the same thing. He answered, "I will, sir," but he did not go.

"'Which of the two did what his father wanted?'

"'The first,' they answered" (Matthew 21:28-31).

The Filter of Faith

Our highest calling is to love God and use that love to serve Him and others. Unfortunately, many of us have neglected to focus on this truth. We have developed unhealthy habits, allowing our emotions to be controlled by other people's attitudes and actions. Our hearts are often damaged as a result.

However, when we filter all aspects of life through the lens of faith and a strong heart governed by God, everything we do flows from that healthy perspective. When we set healthy boundaries in all areas of life, we can make wise, rational, and godly choices that enable us to treat others and ourselves in authentic and loving ways that bring honor and glory to God.

The Blessings of the Past

A wise therapist once told me, "If you don't let your past die, you'll never be able to live."

Lisa Buffaloe, one of my questionnaire respondents, said, "We can either allow our past to consume us or allow God's healing so we can move forward. It's about taking thoughts captive and dealing with the past through God's gentle touch."

Taking thoughts captive. I like how that sounds.

Looking forward can sometimes be difficult, especially if our personal struggles have included pain and adversity. Perhaps the trauma of a difficult past never really leaves you. You may still feel helpless and perhaps even fear for your life. But our immediate choice to derail those negative thoughts can make all the difference in the world. Even more important is our ability to change our perception of the past. We can reinterpret painful experiences as blessings.

The important thing to understanding is that God can use all of our experiences and lessons to make a difference in our lives and in the lives of others.

God helped me see that I could process and overcome the negative aspects of trial and tribulation by quickly releasing any negative thought, feeling, or memory and then intentionally viewing the burden as a blessing. Today, when painful memories of my past unexpectedly flood my mind, I stop for a moment and thank God for the life He has given to me now as a result of those experiences. As I see my life from God's perspective, I can see clearly the blessings of empathy and empowerment that have come from all the burdens. However, this process didn't come naturally. It has been an intentional action.

Women have cried enough tears to fill an ocean, and the Bible says, "Those who sow in tears will reap with songs of joy. Those who go out weeping, carrying seed to sow, will return with songs of joy, carrying sheaves with them" (Psalm 126:5-6).

The joy of the Lord is ours to claim! And His Word says, "Blessed are those who have learned to acclaim you, who walk in the light of your presence, LORD. They rejoice in your name all day long; they celebrate your righteousness" (Psalm 89:15-16).

Finding peace isn't an elusive dream. It's really all about perspective and choice.

As we become more aware of our emotions and motivations and identify the areas we know God wants us to change with His help, we have the power to derail the negative thoughts and behavior that controlled us in the past. We have the power to release negative thoughts and behavior at any time and replace them with alternative responses. Healthier and saner responses.

Author and evangelist Hannah Whitall Smith viewed burdens—even the challenging people in her life—as blessings.

> Seeing God in everything is the only thing that will make me loving and patient with people who annoy and trouble me. Then I will see others as the instruments God uses to accomplish His tender and wise purpose for me, and I will even find myself inwardly thanking them for the blessing they have become to me.[1]

Reclaim Your Dreams

What would you be doing in your perfect world? When we have boundary-related challenges, we have often neglected who we are at our core—which is exactly what Satan wants us to do. The enemy wants to render us as ineffective as possible. What better way than to get us to willingly give up our dreams and the calling or gifts God has given us?

Alas, not every dream from our past can come true. If you're 65 years old and you've always dreamed of being a prima ballerina with an international company, you probably won't realize this particular dream. But what's keeping you from enrolling in a ballet class at a local dance school? From experiencing the joy of expressing yourself through dance?

Laurie, age 59, always dreamed of working at a fashion magazine. That never happened, but today she enjoys discussing fashion on her blog and sharing photos on her Pinterest page.

> We need not be satisfied with simply overcoming the pain of our past. God says we are more than conquerors, which means He has more planned for us to do!

Susan left corporate America to travel the back roads of the United States on a Harley with her retired husband.

Margaret is taking pottery classes at a local community college.

Now in her sixties, Elizabeth has become a hairdresser.

What do you *really* want to do? Ultimately, what we want is for God's truth to be revealed to us. We want to see His goodness and love in all of the circumstances in our lives—past and present—and to give Him honor and glory as we ask Him to reveal His plans and purposes for our lives.

Use your notebook and write down your dreams, your goals, your vision. Then begin to pray about them. How can God use your past and your present—your SANITY journey—to make a difference?

We need not be satisfied with simply overcoming the pain of our past. God says we are more than conquerors, which means He has more planned for us to do! I believe God wants us to savor the blessings that have come from our past and to recognize the ways He has prepared us for such a time as this.

I trust God when He tells us, "You will go out in joy and be led forth in peace; the mountains and hills will burst into song before you, and all the trees of the field will clap their hands" (Isaiah 55:12).

Can there be a more glorious promise than that? The trees are clapping their hands!

God wants us to stop bearing the burdens of our past and start bearing the fruit.

We are all instruments in His plan, and He is just waiting to share all of His plans with us—if only we can stop long enough to be still in body and mind and truly know in our hearts that He alone is God. If only we will choose to walk in His power and authority.

When we are in God's presence, we can hear Him say our name, and in this sweet whisper of love, we find peace and true sanity.

A Final Word from Allison

There is a growing sense of urgency in my spirit to issue a wake-up call to women who realize their lives are spinning out of control yet find themselves powerless to do anything about it.

Virtually everywhere I go, I see people caught-up in the insanity that propels life when boundaries are weak or non-existent, when relationships are out of priority. Times when our inability to take control in a God-honoring way has sent us on a course of discouragement and even self-destruction. We live in an increasingly toxic world, and Satan has a very clear agenda—to kill, steal, and destroy. The enemy does not want us to be effective women in any areas of life, but especially in spreading the gospel message of Christ. The evil one doesn't want us to take control, or to find peace and sanity—he wants to convince us that living on the gerbil wheel of insanity is our lot in life.

Sisters, it's time to put our feet down and stomp on the lies and destruction of the enemy. We can influence our world in powerful and positive ways when we know our identity in Christ, and walk boldly with confidence and purpose.

It's time for us to claim the resurrection power and spiritual authority of Jesus, and to use that power to change and transform our life and the lives of others. It's time to walk in truth and stand in victory. The sooner we plant the seeds of SANITY in our hearts, the sooner our harvests will grow, and our lives will bear fruit.

When we do our best, God will do the rest.

You, too, can find SANITY, set healthy boundaries, and take back your life. Remember, God will always make a way where there seems to be no way. He is the author of our U-turns, new beginnings, and healthy boundaries!

God bless and keep you!

Allison

The SANITY Support Creed

I cannot change the life of another person regardless of how much I would like him or her to change. However, I can change myself and the choices I make. Beginning today I am going to consistently focus on making intentional choices based on love and not on guilt, fear, or anger. Beginning today, I will set healthy boundaries by choosing daily to follow the Six Steps to SANITY. I will no longer accept responsibility for the choices other people make. I will learn how to be firm and loving at the same time. I will affirm that God does some of His best work through our pain. I will let God do a good work in me and through me as I learn to guard my heart and take control in a way that honors God and fulfills the call He has placed on my life.

I will gain SANITY and find the peace that transcends all understanding.

SettingBoundariesBooks.com

Appendix 2

Developing Your Action Plan

You've been reading a long time, and I hope you've digested the previous chapters in light of your own situation. Now it's time to take the next big step. It's time to write down your goals. No more excuses. Remember the "N" Step in SANITY: *Nip Excuses in the Bud*!

Let's begin by getting specific about your written action plan. As you start, remember that...

1. Unless you're developing a document to present to someone whose life and livelihood your new boundaries will directly affect, your action plan is currently for your eyes only. This exercise is designed to help you identify challenging areas, develop new habits, and be aware of the possible consequences of your new choices. For more information on developing action plans for adult children, dysfunctional aging parents, difficult people, and even for yourself insofar as challenges with food and losing weight, see the applicable Setting Boundaries® book on that subject. (A list appears at the end of this book.)

2. As you change your own negative behavior into more firm and loving responses, speak the truth. Don't mislead others

with wishy-washy answers. This isn't fair and may give others false hopes. If you don't learn how to say yes with authenticity and no with conviction, others will take you for granted and lose respect for you.

3. If you are by definition a giver (a fixer or doer), the people who are close to you may not be capable of granting you support. But that doesn't mean supportive people aren't out there. Find them. Remember the "A" Step in SANITY: *Assemble Supportive People*.

Developing a written plan of action that helps us stay spiritually on track and explains the consequences of our actions is a critical component of SANITY.

Healthy relationships can fill our lives with joy, comfort, and satisfaction. Conversely, unhealthy relationships can burden our hearts with sadness, pain, and confusion. Thankfully, many unhealthy relationships can become healthy with the right care—the right prescription.

The SANITY Steps can be the medication we need to heal our unhealthy relationships, beginning with our own hearts. They can be the tools God uses to help you become the person He wants you to be. They can also be helpful tools for others in your life, but remember, that choice isn't yours to make. You can only change you regardless of how much you want someone else to change. Therefore, this written plan is all about taking control of what you *can* control.

God can change others through us if He chooses to.

Learning to Be Firm and Loving

Other people may become confused when we change the rules in the middle of the game. When we experience a change of heart or perspective during a relationship, those we care about can be unsettled. The person we are becoming is not the person they used to know.

Developing a written plan of action can help to prepare us to navigate the sometimes rough waters of change. It helped Pam.

Pam is a new believer. After years of feeling an all-consuming emptiness in her heart and soul, Pam chose to *Yield Everything to God* (the "Y" Step in SANITY), and her life changed. However, her husband and extended family don't share her newfound faith or her new perspective on boundaries, so Pam has realized that she needs to develop a written plan. It isn't to present to them, but to help clarify her own feelings and to guide her in making God-honoring choices and changes.

Before she made her U-turn toward God, Pam and her husband were known as being premiere party hosts with the perfect party house. But now, this has become a significant area of conflict in their marriage because Pam has begun to feel increasingly uncomfortable hosting these raucous gatherings at their home.

"I'm hardly a prude, but the level of alcohol being consumed at our parties is significant," she says. "I frequently find myself hiding people's car keys and paying for cabs. I'm taking care of people who aren't taking responsibility for themselves."

When Pam began to look at the lifestyle she and her husband, Steve, were encouraging and sometimes even funding, she felt convicted that something wasn't right. The more Pam prayed for wisdom and discernment about this, the more she was able to *Trust the Voice of the Spirit* (the "T" Step in SANITY). Eventually, she realized it was wrong to continue this enabling behavior.

"At first I tried laying down the law and obstinately told Steve, 'No more parties here!' Steve said that I was going crazy and that he had no intention of joining me, and we had quite a shouting match over it. It took me a few days of pouting and stomping around the house before I realized I was being unreasonable in my expectation that Steve should suddenly share my conviction. I had a change of heart, and I'm seeing things from a different perspective, but that doesn't give me the right to tell him what he can and can't do in his own home. Although

I think he does need to change his thinking and perspective, I can't make him change, and it isn't my place to try to make him change. I was ashamed that the face of God I showed him was judgmental, angry, and unloving."

The Holy Spirit convicted Pam that if she wanted to implement change, she needed to set healthy boundaries with firmness *and* love.

The Consequences of Conviction

Unfortunately, Pam's new lifestyle choices have caused a great deal of friction in her relationship with Steve, who is resistant to change and refuses to attend marriage counseling to discuss their increasingly differing expectations.

However, as she continued to *Yield Everything to God* (the "Y" Step in SANITY), Pam boldly claimed the power to walk in God's authority and let Him help her overcome all obstacles. Pam has intentionally said goodbye to insanity. She knows that God has transformed her life, and she believes He has called her to witness to her family and others. She's not always certain how to do that effectively, but she's trusting God to show her the way.

Pam is currently seeing a Christian counselor to help her learn to set healthy boundaries with her unbelieving family and to communicate her needs in a firm and loving manner—a God-honoring way. As part of that counseling, Pam is doing a lot of writing in order to eventually *Implement an Action Plan* (the "I" Step in SANITY). She is depending on her written plan to reflect God's will for her life and to help her stay accountable.

So grab your notebook and let's get started on the "I" Step in SANITY as you *Implement an Action Plan*. We reach a landmark moment in our lives when we can calmly and rationally give voice to our needs, even if that voice begins on paper for our eyes only.

Your action plan will consist of eight tasks divided into three sections.

Creating an Action Plan

Get Ready

1. Identify what isn't working.

2. Identify what needs to be done to make it work.

3. Identify what needs to happen first.

Get Set

4. Consider the consequences.

5. Consider asking someone to help.

6. Rehearse/practice.

Go!

7. Take action.

8. Be consistent.

Get Ready

Any relationship involves certain mutual needs, requirements, and expectations. Love (romantic love or Christian brotherly/sisterly love), respect, responsibility, and the like should be happening in a good, meaningful flow between two people for the relationship to be functioning. What specific things are interrupting that flow in your life? Getting ready is all about identifying...

- what isn't working
- what needs to be done to make it work
- what needs to happen first

Start your action plan by making a list of what isn't working in your life. It's important to clearly state the specific issue. Otherwise, the situation can become so broad and general that nothing effective can ever be done. To say, "My boss is an idiot" or "My neighbor is crazy" may help you blow off steam, but it won't help you to identify what's really going on or understand whether you need to set a healthy boundary. Be more definitive: "My boss has unreasonable expectations about working overtime," or "I work from home, and my neighbor has two small dogs that bark nonstop all day when she is at work."

Don't worry about prioritizing your list at this point. Just write down in your notebook what isn't working as concisely as possible. Here are some examples.

- My husband refuses to do housework even though we both work full-time.

- My best friend at church often gossips.

- I can't depend on my ex-husband to be reliable and responsible.

- I don't know how to say no when I'm asked to volunteer.

- My coworker steals office supplies.

- My husband hits me.

- My sister is a chronic enabler and interferes in my life.

- My boyfriend is jealous of my friends.

- A neighbor has a dog that barks almost 24/7.

- My ex-wife makes custody issues a nightmare.

- My roommate leaves the doors unlocked and windows open when he leaves the house.

- My father-in-law swears profusely around my young children.

- My husband watches Internet pornography every day.

- My adult child is addicted to drugs, and his lifestyle causes drama, chaos, and crisis in our family.

Sometimes our struggle is with ourselves, as in the example, "I don't know how to say no when I'm asked to volunteer." But the majority of what isn't working in a boundary-challenged life will usually involve other people as the list above attests.

Taking the time to identify your issues will prepare you to make God-honoring responses. The way you respond to these people when they push your buttons will make all the difference in the world.

Once your list is complete, it's important to pick the battles that matter the most. Review your list carefully and prioritize three issues to approach first.

For example, Pam had more than a dozen items on her first list. She wrote down everything she could think of that wasn't working in her life, from issues with her husband and son to relationships with her siblings. In reviewing her list and praying about it, she was ultimately able to *Trust the Voice of the Spirit* (the "T" Step in SANITY) and identify her top three priorities.

This is a critical point to remember as you move forward to make any boundary-related changes. Always take the time to stop, be still, and pray about your steps. Pick up your Bible and read it. Search for passages applicable to your circumstances, follow an established Bible study guide, or ask God to direct you where He would have you go and randomly open your Bible and read. Take the time to interpret what you are reading in relation to your current life circumstances.

Be intentional about asking the Lord to use the Word of God to shine much-needed light on your life. And then remember to *Trust the Voice of the Spirit* (the "T" Step in SANITY).

This is Pam's top-three list of what wasn't working in her life:

- My husband doesn't share my belief in God.
- I now see things as sin that I used to find acceptable.
- Some unbelieving family and friends are antagonistic about my new faith, the church, and the Bible. They

frequently misquote or misinterpret Scripture to paint it in a bad light.

Once we've identified what isn't working, we need to identify what needs to be done to make it work, and then identify what needs to happen first. In Pam's case, her priority issue is that her husband does not share her belief system. Ideally, she would love for her husband to give his life to Christ, and that may very well happen. However, in the meantime she's facing some rather challenging choices and to help her identify what needs to be done to make it work, and what needs to happen first, are issues she's discussing with a licensed Christian counselor.

Get Set

Now that we've identified our top-three issues to focus on first, let's take a close look at two kinds of consequences:

1. The *unknown* consequences that *may* come as a result of making new choices.
2. The *defined* consequences that *will* come if a boundary is violated.

Let's begin with the first aspect.

A wise woman will apply the "S" Step in SANITY and stop, step back, and consider the possible consequences of the new choices she is going to make.

The law of gravity says that what goes up must come down. Likewise, when we begin to set healthy boundaries and change our behavior, attitudes, and responses, consequences will be inevitable. Some of those consequences may be fluid and flexible, others frustrating and frightening. Either way, never doubt that consequences are a certainty. The question is, will you be prepared for them?

For example, when Marie greeted Scott at the door that first night with a prayer, he could have responded in any number of ways. She prayed that he would be receptive (and he was). However, she had explored virtually every possible consequence beforehand so she could be prepared. He could yell and storm out of the house, he could get angry and not talk to her, he could become defensive and critical, or he could disregard her sincerity and laugh it off.

The consequences on Elizabeth's list were very serious. She knew that if she set firm boundaries with her son regarding his alcoholism and violence, the possibilities were frightening. He could fly off the handle and abuse her or his brother. He could even kill them in a fit of rage. Or he could kill himself in a depressed state of sadness. He could also injure or kill someone else with his drunken driving, or burn her house down, or...the list went on and on.

"Considering these possibilities made me sad, but even so, this exercise was very empowering and helpful to me," Elizabeth said. "I may have been shaking in my boots at times, but I was prepared, ready, and rational. It was time."

The more prepared we are, the better.

We tend to think of consequences as the bad things that happen when we make mistakes or poor choices. A traffic ticket is the consequence of exceeding the speed limit. Being arrested is the consequence of driving while intoxicated.

However, consequences can also be positive, so consider that as you write. For example, let's say we're physically out of shape. Negative consequences would include poor circulation, stiff joints, and being overweight. So we start exercising and eating better. Consequences of those two actions include losing weight, moving with more ease, and perhaps even sleeping better. As you feel and look better, this increased confidence and energy could propel you to go back to school and train for a new career. The positive consequence of that could be a great new job, an increase in income, and a total change of lifestyle...all from exercising and eating better!

We've also learned that our thoughts, feelings, habits, and unrealistic expectations all can have consequences. For example, we may have an unrealistic expectation that we can all look like stick-thin supermodels on the pages of glossy high-fashion magazines. Consequences of this unreasonable expectation can include feelings of inadequacy, shame, unworthiness, and guilt. We experience consequences even without consciously thinking about them or preparing for them.

So consequences can be negative or positive and can tumble into one another and cause an avalanche effect. For example, if we don't go to work, we don't get paid. If we don't get a paycheck, we can't pay our bills. If we don't pay our bills, we lose our car, home, and belongings. When we lose our home, we must find somewhere else to live, and... you can see how the avalanche effect happens.

When we live a reasonably sane life with healthy emotions and boundaries, positive consequences tend to come naturally as a result of good choices and right relationships. However, that is typically not the case when we've had weak or nonexistent boundaries. Many of us have been caught up in the drama, chaos, and crisis that occur in our relationships, and we're always putting out the fires of consequences instead of preparing for them.

Defining a Specific Consequence

Now let's a take a look at specific consequences associated with a boundary we are putting into place.

Boundaries have meaning only if consequences result when they're violated. If there is no real consequence, the boundary is faulty.

The consequence of a violated boundary needs to be determined when the boundary is set. When you *Implement an Action Plan*, you need to make it all-inclusive. You need to intentionally look at the big picture—your vision must include your consequences. You might need to establish consequences for yourself, or you might have to verbally articulate them to another person.

For example, when you tell your teenager you expect her to be home by her curfew time, you've established a reasonable boundary, and an appropriate consequence must be attached to it in case it is violated. Your daughter needs to be aware of that consequence before the fact.

Identifying reasonable expectations and communicating them in a firm and loving manner is healthy. It isn't selfish or rude.

Establishing an appropriate and reasonable consequence is critical. Herein lays the challenge for many women.

Sadly, some of us haven't followed through with appropriate consequences, and that choice has consequences of its own. When we don't follow through with consequences, we set a precedent. Other people learn that we really don't mean what we say.

For example, when Elizabeth first presented her son with the new house rules, he laughed them off, never expecting her to actually follow them. He began to take her seriously when he came home from work the day after one of his drunken rampages and discovered the locks had been changed on the house.

When we set boundaries, it's important that we mean what we say each step of the way. We must present a clearly defined boundary, include reasonable consequences, note violations of the boundary, and follow through with the consequences.

Coming up with a clearly defined consequence is hard for many of us. This is another area where supportive people can help you. Ask them to help you design a fitting consequence for a violated boundary. When you think you've reached a dead end with your boundary issues, you'll be surprised at how creative your supporters can be.

Make sure that your consequences are realistic for you and for the other party, that they're designed to bring about the proper behavior, and that you follow through on them. This last point may be hardest of all. When your adult son lands in jail and calls you for help even though you've clearly spelled out the consequences should he be arrested, it will very hard on your mother's heart to do what you've said you'll do. Trust me, I know.

Take the time to practice and rehearse what you are going to say and how you will say it. And definitely take the time to pray about it and listen for Holy Spirit guidance.

Go!

This is the step where we take action. Consistent follow-through may be challenging, but you may be surprised how much easier it is to take action now that you've done all the written preparation and have applied the SANITY Steps to your choices.

When you communicate your expectation (boundary) to your daughter, communicate the consequence too. If she's late, she loses car privileges for two weeks.

Now it's up to your daughter to fulfill her end of the bargain, and it's up to you to say what you mean and mean what you say in a firm and loving way.

It's important to note what "no car privileges" means to you and to your daughter. Does it mean your daughter must be responsible for her own transportation and walk, ride her bike, or take a bus? Does it mean you will pay her bus fare? Or does it mean you will now become a taxi service? What lesson has she really learned from the consequence of missing curfew?

Some consequences need teeth to be truly effective and impactful—and not just consequences associated with our children.

Here are some examples of consequences:

To an unfaithful husband. "I have forgiven you for your unfaithfulness because you tell me you have repented and want to save our marriage. But to guard my heart and to help you be accountable—for your own good as well as mine—the consequence of another episode of unfaithfulness will be a divorce." (Do not issue this consequence unless you mean it.)

A wife whose husband has been unfaithful is entirely within her rights to include these items in her new boundary:

- testing for an STD

- no working late at night
- mandatory counseling

To a coworker who has made improper advances. "If you touch me again, I will file a formal complaint with Human Resources."
To a teen who doesn't respect your curfew. "If you stay out past the appointed time again, you will not be able to go out on the weekends at all until you have proven yourself trustworthy."
To yourself. "If I eat dessert tonight in violation of my diet, I will have to spend an additional 30 minutes on the treadmill tomorrow."

When Enough Is Enough

Estelle has been letting a coworker take advantage of her for months, and she's finally reached the end of her rope. She wants to find SANITY, and she knows it's time to practice the first step: *Stop Your Own Negative Behavior.* She's also in a rut at work and has decided it's time to stop settling for mediocrity in her professional life. In fact, she filled an entire page in her steno pad with things she wants to stop at work:

- Stop my own negative behavior and responses to my coworker.
- Stop my own negative behavior and "safe" responses in all areas of my job.
- Stop working overtime to complete work I didn't accomplish because I was helping my coworker.
- Stop jeopardizing my own job.
- Stop enabling my coworker.
- Stop eating lunch at my desk.
- Stop sitting at my desk during breaks and take a walk outside instead.
- Stop being intimidated by my boss and other coworkers above me.

- Stop treating my job as if I'm in prison and see the future opportunities available.

- Stop thinking I'm too old to go back to school and get more training in order to advance in my company.

She decided earlier to *Assemble Supportive People* and discuss the negative aspects of her people-pleasing personality. She is prepared to *Nip Excuses in the Bud.* She is now ready to *Implement an Action Plan* and to *Trust the Voice of the Spirit* as she intentionally prays for wisdom and discernment about addressing the coworker issue and about her job in general—a job she feels is at a dead end. Estelle understands that she is responsible to establish healthy boundaries with this coworker and that she must not only *Yield Everything to God* but also take control of that which she can control and begin to address this specific situation with her coworker. To do this effectively, Estelle is prepared to do the work to unpack the emotional baggage she has carried for years concerning her unmet needs, emotions, and motivation as well as the years of fruitless labor she has experienced as she's lived on her own gerbil wheel of insanity.

Here is Estelle's list to *Get Ready, Get Set, and Go!* Using the same eight steps, write out your own plan for your top three priority concerns following Estelle's example.

Get Ready

1. Identify what isn't working.

- My coworker keeps giving me her work to do.

- I'm spending way too many hours at work trying to get everything done.

2. Identify what needs to be done to make it work.

- She needs to stop giving me her work to do.

- I need to tell her I cannot do her work.

3. Identify what needs to be done first.

- I need to tell her no the next time she asks.

Get Set

4. Consider the consequences

- She will get angry with me.
- She may refuse to talk to me.
- She could bad-mouth me behind my back.

5. Consider asking someone to help.

- If this doesn't stop, I could go to our supervisor, but I hate to do that.
- I could get feedback from my support group.

6. Rehearse/practice.

- "I would really like to help you with that project, but I need to stay on task with my responsibilities. Perhaps you should discuss it with Mr. Hall?"

Go!

7. Take Action.

- I will change the way I respond to my coworker.
- I will speak with my coworker on our break.

8. Be consistent and follow through.

- I will not be wishy-washy. I will be firm and kind. I will mean what I say and say what I mean.

Do this written exercise as many times as you need to until you have a clear picture of what the issue really is and what needs to happen to make a change. Although this may appear to be the hardest step of all, there is something very freeing about seeing our plans on paper.

As you move forward to communicate your needs verbally, remember the call to express yourself with firmness and love.

As you begin to take control and apply the SANITY Steps, you will find your personal power and strength increasing. This is a natural result of exercising spiritual authority. This self-assurance will enable you to verbally respond in positive and healthy ways in boundary-related situations or circumstances.

When people overstep their boundaries and you choose to assert proper control of the situation, you usually won't have to show these people a written statement of the new boundaries and their consequences. However, that may not always be the case.

Presenting a Written Plan to Someone Else

Sometimes you may need to present another person with a written document that defines new or revised boundaries. For Elizabeth and her son, it included her list of nonnegotiable items, including no drunkenness or destruction of property, as well as specific consequences of infractions. Or you could develop a document in collaboration with another person in order to negotiate and agree on issues of concern. You could also create a contract that you ask someone to sign.

This written statement could be as simple as a Post-it note stuck on the refrigerator that says, "Weekday curfew is ten p.m. or no car for two weeks." This leaves no room for assumption about the time your teenager is expected home and the associated consequences.

Think of this like any document that defines specific rules, regulations, covenants, or such. I recently received a one-page Rules & Regulations document from the sanitation department of my city. It outlined the new rules (boundaries) for trash and recycling. Bins must be stored so they are not visible from the street. They can be placed on the curb after five p.m. on Sunday. If they are not removed within 24 hours of trash pick-up, homeowners will be fined. It was all very clear and included the consequences of not following the rules. Short, sweet, and leaving no room for misinterpretation.

We could alleviate so much confusion by creating written guidelines for situations that are fraught with unclear expectations, accountability, and responsibility.

For example, I talk to a lot of people who are having roommate problems. Whether you're in your twenties sharing an apartment, divorcees sharing a house, or parents who have invited their adult child to return home until he gets back on his feet, if a group of adults are living under your roof, everyone could benefit from a written document that identifies expectations, responsibilities, and the consequences of noncompliance, or boundary-breaking.

When my son was nearing the end of his prison sentence, I considered allowing him to live with me for the duration of his parole. Chris did not ask if he could come stay with me. We lived in different states, and he was thoroughly aware of the boundaries I had established concerning enabling. If you've read the first book in this series, you might think I'm a glutton for punishment. But the truth is, my son had spent many years paying for the crimes he committed, and from his letters and our phone conversations, I could sense a significant change in his attitude. Our relationship had also changed in many ways, and I had most definitely changed.

So I prayed about it, I talked to wise counsel, and I listened to the Spirit. When I was sure I wanted to extend this opportunity to my son, I first sat down and wrote out what I would be able to provide and for how long, what I wouldn't provide, what would be expected of him, and the consequences of noncompliance. Then I developed a written covenant agreement that I mailed to him several months before his release.

"I love you, I believe in you, and I want to extend this offer to you, but you need to be aware of the big picture. If this isn't something you can live with for the duration of your parole, you should make other arrangements for when you are released," I said to him on the phone.

This wasn't a document that he could negotiate. It was a take it or leave it proposition. Still, it was his choice. There were other places he could have lived when released, places where the boundaries would have been much more lenient.

To make a long story short, Chris welcomed the opportunity and agreed to my terms. He lived with me for the duration of his 18-month parole and obtained his own apartment just two weeks before the date he was supposed to move. That season was not without trial and tribulation, but it would have been a nightmare without the clearly defined structure of the action plan and covenant agreement.

The Rewards of Kept Boundaries

Of course, we hope that setting boundaries results in a change in behavior—ours or someone else's. Just as your intended consequences should be clear, so should the rewards. Your support team can help you determine these as well.

Our goal with boundaries is usually a change in behavior, so we need to know what will motivate the person to change the bad behavior. Authentic praise is often one such motivation. Never withhold praise for a job well done. We all thrive on praise. If people with whom you need to set boundaries have heard nothing but criticism (especially from you), they're not very likely to respond well to boundaries unless their compliance brings praise from you. Watch for even the smallest opportunity to praise the offender.

This is true not just for our youth but for anyone, including husbands. Many wives who are justifiably disappointed in the behavior of their husbands have perhaps never realized the power of their words. Men like to hear that their wives love them, respect them, and notice when they're going the extra mile.

Here's a good boundary to set for yourself. Find at least one person a day to whom you can offer praise—perhaps even a courteous sales clerk at the mall.

Likewise, if you tend to be compliant and passive, you may have set a precedent by praising and accepting unacceptable behavior simply because you don't want to rock the boat. A good boundary to set in this instance is to speak up and clearly vocalize a necessary boundary in a calm and rational manner. This may take some practice.

The tone in many homes is set by the woman and can range from passive to aggressive. The key is to find healthy balance between the two extremes—sanity.

Go Forth with SANITY

It's never too late to take control and find SANITY. Regardless of our age, God is not through with us yet!

Now in her forties, Oscar-winning actress Marisa Tomei says she is finally feeling comfortable in her own skin. "No matter what age you are, there are cycles of where you put your energy, things you're trying to let go of and to cultivate. These days, my emphasis is on making more and more heartfelt and authentic decisions. You have to keep your eye on the prize, be more courageous, more connected to life." [1]

We can make an intentional decision to be more courageous. God's Word gives us the strength to get off the gerbil wheel of insanity. "Have I not commanded you? Be strong and courageous. Do not be afraid; do not be discouraged, for the LORD your God will be with you wherever you go" (Joshua 1:9).

Christian Conflict Resolution

Our inability to set healthy boundaries or to follow up with appropriate consequences may result in serious conflict. You may feel the only way you can take action is to seek legal advice and counsel. Resolving conflict in a way that honors God can be challenging in a world where the threat of litigation looms large.

Sometimes an unbeliever takes a believer to court, and you can't do much about that. But it's important to participate with the right kind of spirit. For believers, however, it's different. In 1 Corinthians 6:1-8, Paul makes it clear that Christians are not to take other Christians to court. Unfortunately, the number of lawsuits among believers is considerable.

Yet there is a process described in the Bible to address conflict and disputes in a godly manner.

> Moreover if your brother sins against you, go and tell him his fault between you and him alone. If he hears you, you have gained your brother. But if he will not hear, take with you one or two more, that "by the mouth of two or three witnesses every word may be established." And if he refuses to hear them, tell it to the church. But if he refuses even to hear the church, let him be to you like a heathen and a tax collector (Matthew 18:15-17 NKJV).

Before initiating or responding to any legal action, pray intentionally for wisdom and discernment. Read the Scriptures carefully concerning this issue.

If you're currently facing a lawsuit or would like to protect yourself from a lawsuit in the future, you might consider adding a Christian mediation/arbitration clause to your current contracts. Peacemaker Ministries (www.peacemaker.net) provides Rules of Procedure for Christian Conciliation.

For more information on developing action plans for adult children, dysfunctional aging parents, difficult people, and even your own challenges with food and losing weight, see the applicable Setting Boundaries® book on those subjects. A list appears at the end of this book.

Sample Letters to Send

Drawing on her experience as a Christian counselor, Bernis Riley provided these sample letters for the book *Setting Boundaries® with Difficult People*. You can personalize and mail them or use them as scripts in conversations. Because they are applicable to so many relationship challenges, I have included these letters to help you approach the people in your life you feel God is telling you to communicate with about your new boundaries.

To a Difficult Ex-spouse

Dear _____,

I realize that since our marriage ended, things between us have been hard. I also realize that I have said and done some things that have hurt your feelings and have damaged our relationship. I want you to know that I'm sorry for hurting you and causing harm to our relationship. I want things to change between us, and though I desire that we both change, I cannot make you change. I can only change myself and my responses and reactions to you, so I'm choosing to set some boundaries for the health of this relationship.

From now on, rather than withdrawing from you or attacking you when I feel criticized by you, I will simply let you know that your words have hurt my feelings, and I will ask you to acknowledge my hurt feelings and take back the hurtful words. If you cannot do this, I will not continue that conversation with you. Until you acknowledge the hurtful words or actions, any communication between us will be limited to only what is necessary for exchanging information.

In addition, you are required to follow the judge's ruling in our divorce papers, and if you choose not to abide by that legal document, I will notify my lawyer, and the legal system will enforce those rulings. I sincerely want a good and respectable relationship between us, so that is why I am letting you know what my boundaries are from this time forward.

Sincerely,

_____ Date _____

To a Coworker or Boss

Dear _____,

I want to have a good working relationship with you, and I believe you want the same with me. However, I feel that for that to happen, I need to let you know that several times in the past few weeks [or months], you have crossed what I consider to be personal or professional boundaries with me. For instance, [state a couple of examples to illustrate your point].

In order to work effectively with you, I will not allow boundaries like these to be crossed in the future. If you do continue to violate my personal or professional boundaries, I will find it necessary to file a complaint with Human Resources [or the person's manager]. I would like to speak with you personally about this letter so that I am not misunderstood and so that you can be clear about what I need from you in the future. I would like to arrange a meeting between us and [another coworker or boss] to discuss this issue.

Thank you,

_____ Date _____

To a Difficult Family Member

Dear _____,

I want you to know how important you are to me. I highly value our relationship and want it to be the best it can be.

However, over the past few years [or months], some things have happened between us that I feel have damaged our relationship. [Name a few of those things.]

I don't want these things to come between us and hinder our relationship, but neither can I sit quietly by and not say anything. In the past, I've felt powerless to say anything, but now I realize that you're much too important in my life for me to not try to mend our relationship. I do not hold these things from the past against you, but should something like this happen again, I will [Write your boundary and its consequence. For example, "I will immediately end our conversation if you start calling me names, and I will not have contact with you until you have apologized.]

We both are responsible for the health of this relationship, and this is what I must do to fulfill my part of that responsibility.

Sincerely,

_____ Date _____

To a Difficult Friend

Dear _____,

I want you to understand that I write this letter with great difficulty. Our friendship has meant a great deal to me over the years, and the last thing I want to do is to ruin it. However, some things have happened recently that have me wondering if we can continue to be friends as we once were.

I need you to know up front what some of those things are so you're not wondering about them. [Name the things your friend has done that have harmed you during the friendship.]

I don't think you intentionally wanted to hurt me, but I need you to know that those things did hurt me and made me want to pull away from our friendship.

So in the future, if you [name the offense], I will call your attention to it and will ask you to take responsibility for your behavior. If you cannot do that, I will need to back away from this relationship for my own well-being. I hope you understand and I want to rebuild this relationship into a safe friendship for both of us.

Your friend,

_____ Date _____

To End a Difficult Relationship with a Family Member or Friend

Dear _____,

I have been thinking about our relationship lately and have come to realize that perhaps the best thing for everyone would be for us to no longer have contact with each other until you [apologize for…, admit…, gone for counseling, stopped drinking…].

For my own well-being and that of my [family, children, parents], I'm willing to let this relationship go. We both need to make some changes for the better, but I cannot do that as long as this relationship is in its present state.

I don't know whether you will care that I am taking this step. All I know is that I need to do this for my own sanity and because I do care about you.

Sincerely,

_____ Date _____

Notes

Chapter 3: Are We Helping or Enabling?

1. Henry Cloud and John Townsend, *Boundaries: When to Say Yes, When to Say No to Take Control of Your Life* (Grand Rapids: Zondervan, 1992), 25.

Chapter 5: Why Setting Boundaries Is So Difficult for Christian Women

1. Catherine Clark Kroeger and Mary J. Evans, eds., *The IVP Women's Bible Commentary* (Downers Grove, IL: InterVarsity Press, 2001), xxx-xxxi.

2. Faith Martin, *Call Me Blessed: The Emerging Christian Woman* (Pittsburgh, PA: Spring Valley Press, 1998), 19.

3. Henry T. Blackaby and Claude V. King, *Experiencing God: How to Live the Full Adventure of Knowing and Doing the Will of God* (Nashville, TN: Broadman & Holman, 1994), 194.

Chapter 6: Encountering God's Word and Wisdom

1. Catherine Clark Kroeger and Mary J. Evans, eds., *The IVP Women's Bible Commentary* (Downers Grove, IL: InterVarsity Press, 2001), xxiii.

2. Gretchen Gaebelein Hull, *Equal to Serve: Women and Men Working Together Revealing the Gospel* (Grand Rapids, MI: Baker Books, 2003), 110.

Chapter 7: When Boundaries Are Violated

1. Os Hillman, "Is God Really in Control?," In the Workplace, www.intheworkplace.com/apps/articles/default.asp?blogid=1935&view=post&articleid=80916.

2. Catherine Clark Kroeger and Nancy Nason-Clark, *No Place for Abuse: Biblical and Practical Resources to Counteract Domestic Violence* (Downers Grove, IL: InterVarsity Press, 2010), 169.

3. Catherine Clark Kroeger and James R. Beck, *Healing the Hurting: Giving Hope and Help to Abused Women* (Grand Rapids, MI: Baker Books, 1998), 27.

4. Kroeger and Beck, *Healing the Hurting*, 62.

5. Patrick J. Carnes, *The Betrayal Bond: Breaking Free of Exploitive Relationships* (Deerfield Beach, FL: Health Communications, 1997), 116.

6. June Hunt, *Counseling Through Your Bible: Providing Biblical Hope and Practical Help for 50 Everyday Problems* (Eugene, OR: Harvest House, 2008), 140.

7. Mary J. Evans and Catherine Clark Kroeger, eds., *The Women's Study Bible*, New Living Translation (New York, NY: Oxford University Press, Inc., 2009), 764-65.

8. Cited in Elisabeth L, *Listen to the Hunger* (Center City, MN: Hazeldon Foundation, 1987), 45.

9. Dr. Laura Schlessinger, *Bad Childhood Good Life: How to Blossom and Thrive in Spite of an Unhappy Childhood* (New York, NY: Harper Collins, 2006), 23-24.

Chapter 8: Saying No Without Guilt

1. Tracey Mitchell, *Downside Up: Transform Rejection in Your Golden Opportunity* (Nashville, TN: Thomas Nelson, 2013), 12-13.

2. Martha Beck, "Take a Flying Leap," *O, The Oprah Magazine*, January 2013, 44.

3. Henry T. Blackaby and Claude V. King, *Experiencing God: How to Live the Full Adventure of Knowing and Doing the Will of God* (Nashville, TN: Broadman & Holman, 1994), 223-24.

Chapter 9: Expectations Can Be Exhausting

1. Dr. Jill Hubbard, *The Secrets Women Keep: What Women Hide and the Truth that Brings Them Freedom* (Nashville, TN: Thomas Nelson, 2008), 7.

Chapter 10: Personality, Emotions, and Motivations

1. Florence Littauer, *Personality Plus: How to Understand Others by Understanding Yourself* (Grand Rapids, MI: Fleming H. Revell, 1983), 11.

2. Donna Carter, *10 Smart Things Women Can Do to Build a Better Life* (Eugene, OR: Harvest House, 2007), 29.

3. Harriet Lerner, *The Dance of Anger: A Woman's Guide to Changing the Patterns of Intimate Relationships* (New York, NY: Perennial Currents, 2005), 1.

4. Allison Bottke, *Setting Boundaries® with Food* (Eugene, OR: Harvest House, 2012), 104.

Chapter 11: Peace, Not Passivity

1. Dr. Jill Hubbard, *The Secrets Women Keep: What Women Hide and the Truth that Brings Them Freedom* (Nashville, TN: Thomas Nelson, 2008), 9.

2. Hubbard, *The Secrets Women Keep*, 8.

Chapter 12: The Fruit of Healthy Boundaries

1. Leslie Vernick, *The Truth Principle* (Eugene, OR: Harvest House, 2000), 20.

2. June Hunt, *How to Rise Above Abuse: Victory for Victims of Five Types of Abuse* (Eugene, OR: Harvest House, 2010), 171.

3. Henry T. Blackaby and Claude V. King, *Experiencing God: How to Live the Full Adventure of Knowing and Doing the Will of God* (Nashville, TN: Broadman & Holman, 1994), 37.

4. June Hunt, *Seeing Yourself Through God's Eyes: A 31-day Devotional Guide* (Eugene, OR: Harvest House, 2008), 11.

5. Jill Briscoe, *Women Who Changed Their World: How God Uses Women to Make a Difference* (Wheaton, IL: Victor Books, 1991), 58.

Chaper 13: Go for It, Girl!

1. Cited in L.B. Cowman, *Streams in the Desert*, ed. Jim Reimann (Grand Rapids, MI: Zondervan, 1997), 353.

Appendix 2: Developing Your Action Plan

1. Margot Dougherty, "Marisa Tomei Profile," *More Magazine*, December 2012–January 2013, 80.

About the Author

Allison Bottke is the author of the popular Setting Boundaries® series, including *Setting Boundaries® with Your Adult Children,* and the general editor of the God Allows U-Turns® series and the God Answers Prayer series. She has written or edited more than 28 nonfiction and fiction books. Allison is a frequent guest on national radio and TV programs and has been featured on *Focus on the Family, The 700 Club, The Dr. Laura Show, Good Morning Texas, Decision Today,* and others.

Visit her at AllisonBottke.com or
SettingBoundariesBooks.com
E-mail Allison at Allison@AllisonBottke.com

HARVEST HOUSE PUBLISHERS
EUGENE, OREGON

Coming Soon from Allison Bottke and Harvest House Publishers…

Setting Boundaries® for Young Women

How many times have you said, "If only I knew then what I know now, things would have been different"? Do you have a special young woman in your life who's facing challenging choices; perhaps a daughter, granddaughter, niece, or the child of a friend? If so, this is your opportunity to influence the young women in your life with a compelling and relevant resource written especially for today's Generation Y Millennials, ages 13-17.

Although the world today is quite different than it was when we were girls, there are still similarities in many issues of the heart that influence the choices we make. Young women are still searching to understand their purpose and place, still searching to be accepted and loved, and they still long to make a difference in their world.

Setting Boundaries® for Young Women will incorporate the Six Steps to SANITY throughout the chapters, as tools young women can use to help them understand, set and maintain healthy boundaries. They will learn that setting a healthy boundary isn't just a temporary plan to put in place when something goes wrong, but is also a necessary aspect of everyday living in developing healthy self-control, independence, and living in a way that honors God. Some of the topics addressed will be; peer pressure, bullying, dating, sexuality, technology, responsibilities, consequences, teen suicide and depression, parental authority, and more.

It's been said, "If we don't stand for something, we'll fall for anything." In a world that preaches the need to tolerate all lifestyle choices, it's important for young people to embrace their Christianity as a lifestyle choice—to stand boldly in their identity and purpose and to walk confidently and courageously with the authority of God.

I invite you to join me in sharing the life-changing message of SANITY with a generation of young women who long to feel protected, safe, significant, and loved.

Setting Boundaries® for Young Women
July 1, 2014

SettingBoundariesBooks.com

Other books in Allison's Setting Boundaries® series...

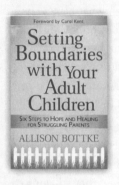

Setting Boundaries® with Your Adult Children:
Six Steps to Hope and Healing
for Struggling Parents

This important and compassionate book will help parents and grandparents of the many adult children who continue to make life painful for their loved ones. Writing from firsthand experience, Allison identifies the lies that kept her and her son in bondage—and how she overcame them. Additional real-life stories from other parents are woven through the text.

A tough-love book to help you cope with dysfunctional adult children, *Setting Boundaries® with Your Adult Children* will empower your family by offering hope and healing through SANITY—a six-step program to help you regain control in your home and in your life.

Setting Boundaries® with Your Aging Parents:
Finding Balance Between Burnout and Respect

This important book will help adult children who long for a better relationship with their parents but feel trapped in a never-ending cycle of chaos, crisis, or drama. With keen insight and a passion to empower adult children, Allison charts a trustworthy roadmap through the often unfamiliar territory of setting boundaries with parents while maintaining personal balance and avoiding burnout. Through the use of professional advice, true stories, and scriptural truth, you will learn how to apply the Six Steps to SANITY.

Setting Boundaries® with Difficult People:
Six Steps to SANITY
for Challenging Relationships

Continuing her Setting Boundaries® series, Allison offers her distinctive Six Steps to SANITY to everyone who must deal with difficult people.

Whether the difficult person is a spouse, in-law, boss, coworker, family member, neighbor, or friend, you will learn how to use these six steps to reset appropriate boundaries and take back your life…for good.

Setting Boundaries® with Food:
Six Steps to Lose Weight, Gain Freedom,
and Take Back Your Life

This is a very personal book for Allison. She knows from personal experience about the struggle against obesity—feeling trapped in a seemingly never-ending cycle of dieting, deprivation, and despair. At one time in her life, Allison's scale hit the 300-pound mark. Her overweight status resulted in Allison being the first full-figure model ever signed by the prestigious Wilhelmina modeling agency, where she worked for some of the biggest names in fashion, such as Gloria Vanderbilt and Alfred Angelo.

From her struggle, Allison offers more than just hope for the future. By introducing her popular SANITY steps, she encourages you to turn away from the insanity of dieting and deprivation and to focus instead on establishing healthy relationships with food, self, others, and God. Her words will strike a chord if you have struggled for years to lose weight as you are encouraged to examine the emotional and spiritual aspects of your bondage to food and obsession with weight.

To learn more about Harvest House books and
to read sample chapters, log on to our website:

www.harvesthousepublishers.com

HARVEST HOUSE PUBLISHERS
EUGENE, OREGON